Beginning Bicycle Racing

Beginning Bicycle Racing

Fast Riding for Fitness and Competition

Fred Matheny

VELO-NEWS
Brattleboro, Vermont

This book is for my wife Deb,
whose support, enthusiasm and perceptive comments
have made both my riding and writing possible.

Third edition, second printing: August 1988
Third edition, first printing: October 1987
Second edition, fourth printing: June 1986
Second edition, third printing: December 1985
Second edition, second printing: May 1985
Second edition, first printing: May 1983
First edition, second printing: June 1982
First edition, first printing: November 1981

Photos copyright © 1987 by: Michael Chritton: pages 12, 18, 24 (top and bottom), 39, 50, 53, 56, 75, 87, 89, 156, 168, 174, 200, 205, 219; Frank Conlon: pages 158, 193; John de Pater: pages 124, 131, 215; Robert F. George: pages 42, 72, 82, 98, 117, 149; Judy Kagay: page 93; Deb Matheny: page 5; Tom Moran: pages 6, 145, 165, 166, 182, 187, 226, 230; Ed Oudenaarden: pages 24 (middle), 102; Cor Vos: pages 31, 108. 132. 170, 172, 180.

ISBN 0-941950-14-X
Library of Congress Catalog Card Number: 87-050802

About The Author

Fred Matheny was born September 16, 1945, and grew up in Ohio. After a high school sports career which included football, basketball and track, he earned an athletic scholarship to Baldwin-Wallace College. While there he lettered for three years on the gridiron as a guard, was selected to the all-league team and was honored as his school's outstanding offensive lineman.

After moving to Colorado in 1970, Matheny became an avid cross-country and downhill skier, backpacker and mountaineer. He also took up running and cycling, dedicating himself to the latter beginning in 1976. He became a Category II Senior midway through his second full season and is now a nationally ranked Veteran, having qualified to ride both the time trial and road race at the National Championships in 1981.

Professionally, Matheny teaches advanced placement senior English at Montrose High School and is chairman of the English department. In addition, he is an instructor of graduate courses in English at Western State College. His wife Debbie, also a teacher, runs, cycles, skis and helps him with his manuscripts. Their son Ross enjoys swimming and gymnastics.

Matheny cycles as much as 9,000 miles a year and races whenever he can. He usually trains alone and has used all the workout methods in this book. He owns several well-used bikes, swears that cycling is a cure-all for a variety of human maladies, and hopes to ride, race and write about the sport for the rest of his life.

In the interest of simpler sentence structures and readability this book is written in the masculine gender, thus avoiding such clutter as *he/she, himself/herself,* etc. This is done in full recognition that American women, though making up less than 10% of our licensed racers, have nevertheless led the way for the U.S. in World Championship competition. Since 1969, road race gold medals have been won by Audrey McElmury and Beth Heiden. On the track Sheila Young-Ochowicz and Connie Paraskevin-Young have each won three match sprint titles and Sue Novara-Reber two. Rebecca (Twigg) Whitehead has won the pursuit title three times and Connie Carpenter-Phinney once. Also, Carpenter-Phinney and Whitehead placed first and second in the Olympic road race in 1984. Above, Janelle Parks celebrates her silver medal ride in the 1986 world road championship.

CONTENTS

PART I
Introduction

PART II
Machinery

PART III
Training

PART IV
Racing

AFTERWORD

Preface
to the Third Edition

As I write this, it is May 1987. It has been nearly seven years since the publication of the first edition of *Beginning Bicycle Racing,* and more than eight years since most of the material for that first edition was written. Six printings and three editions later, I find myself reflecting on how the sport has changed. And, human nature being what it is, on how I've changed, too.

Numbers first. In 1981 the U.S. Cycling Federation listed about 10,000 licensed racers. Now the figure is in excess of 23,000 and growing. Last weekend I raced the Iron Horse, a Memorial Day tradition in Durango, Colorado. The course from Durango to Silverton is 50 miles and 5,000 vertical feet of some of the most spectacular mountain roads this side of the Alps. When I first rode it in 1976, 45 riders started in the combined Category III-IV pack. Now two Category IV fields with limits of 110 each are needed to handle new riders. I don't recall a Veterans race in 1976. This year 95 riders in the 35- to 45-year-old age group left Durango and headed north. More than 900 cyclists raced in all categories and hundreds more rode the tours that accompanied the racing.

Increased racers mean increased exposure. In 1981 not many of my non-cycling friends understood how I spent my leisure time. They didn't know Columbus tubing from Christopher. Now they are buying bikes and asking me sophisticated questions about gears, frame angles, and training.

Media exposure has increased too. In 1981 you couldn't see bike racing on TV. Now coverage of the Tour de France, Paris-Roubaix, and the Race Across America graces major networks. In the ultimate tribute, bike racing is even featured in commercials.

Increased participation has caused problems. The turnover rate in Category IV is one. Many novice riders, too inexperienced to stay upright and have fun in their first race, quickly leave the sport. There is talk of a Category V to ease the transition to competition. Confrontations between motorists and the swelling army of cyclists are increasing. Restrictive laws have been proposed in Colorado and other states with high densities of cyclists. It's harder to find suitable race venues. At the Colorado time trial championships this year, we had to warm up on wind trainers because the police would only allow competitors on the road.

Cycling has become a technological sport. In 1981 there were no heart rate monitors, step-in pedals, disk wheels, or aero brake levers. Hardshell helmets were hot, the selection was limited, and real racers didn't wear them. They did wear wool shorts and jerseys. The bikes of choice were Masis or Colnagos. Cleats were nailed into leather soles.

I've changed too. I'm older, for one thing — funny how that sneaked up on me when I wasn't noticing. In 1980 I was a Category II Senior. Now I'm a Senior 35-45 and I'm growing out of that category. Although I'm not getting any faster, thanks to improved training methods I'm holding my own. But after 12 years of competition, I'm not as interested in long drives to 45-minute criteriums, or killing myself to win, or hammering hills in training until I'm blind. More and more I prefer low-key races, local time trials, hard weekend rides, or cruising up jeep roads on my mountain bike. I want my 7,000-8,000 miles a year to keep me fit and strong. I want to have fun on the bike.

At Durango the hills were as steep as ever, the air as thin at 11,000 feet. It was snowing lightly at the summit of Molas Pass. Loosely pinned numbers cracked in the wind on 50 m.p.h. descents. And in the post-race camaraderie, everyone had a story or an excuse — a close call, the wrong gears, not enough miles. Some things don't change.

Montrose, Colorado
May 26, 1987

PART
I

Introduction

Training rides get a person out in the sun and wind and make the senses more alert than during the rest of the day. This can become an addiction that is life-giving and life-enhancing.

1
Confessions
of a Bike Racer

*I am hooked on an exotic
and exhausting sport—join me*

I AM OFTEN asked three questions by beginning cyclists. On a basic level they want to know what bicycle racing is all about — what are the events like, what are the physical demands, what other sports can it be compared to? Then, because racing seems so exotic and difficult, they ask why I do it. Finally, they wonder about the nature of the much-publicized "positive addiction." Does a person become so involved in cycling that he develops some sort of dependence on the activity?

I used to consider these questions unrelated, unimportant, and the last perhaps a little frivolous. However, the more I've thought about it the more apparent it has become that they are not only related on the deepest level of participation in bike racing, but their answers are central to the whole cycling experience.

Most of what is written about racing tends to deal with the technical aspects. Perhaps it is time now to look at cycling's reason for being and to provide a fuller answer to these questions that have been treated so cursorily in the past.

Sports psychologist William Glasser calls running and other endurance sports "positive addictions." By this he means that a dependence on endurance sports is similar to an addiction to drugs, but the physical and mental results are beneficial. I would like to agree with his assessment of the benign nature of this type of addiction, but sometimes I have my doubts. When I first encountered his addiction metaphor I considered it overly dramatic; now I find that I have become a vivid example of its effects.

I confess that I am an addict, hopelessly hooked on an expensive, exotic, dangerous and exhausting sport. Like a true drug addict I am no longer in control of my participation. I finish long races drained of energy, fluids, glucose and inspiration, but the next day I am out on the road grinding away again. Although these physical demands aren't as destructive as those of narcotic addiction, they are impressive enough to make me question the positive nature of my dependence.

At cycling's top level the demands defy the imagination. The world professional road championship is routinely 150 miles, a distance covered in about six hours. U.S. road events vary from 25 miles to more than 100, depending on the type of race and the classification of the riders. Lung-searing climbs are standard fare in many events, and the ultimate in this department is the annual Bob Cook Memorial Mt. Evans Hill Climb in Colorado. The race begins at about 7,000 feet above sea level in Idaho Springs and climbs 28 torturous miles to over 14,000 feet and the summit. The road is paved all the way, though the surface in the last 10 miles is thin and cracked, so roughened by frost damage that riding it is a little like pedaling up a moguled ski run. A course record was set by Bob Cook at 1 hour and 54 minutes — a time which many tourists would find difficult to equal for 28 miles on the flat. Cook, a thin and bespectacled Olympic team rider, won six races up Mt. Evans before he lost his life to cancer at age 23 in March of 1981.

Even tougher are the multi-day stage races where endurance demands are like no other in the world. A stage race is simply a series of indiviual races on consecutive days. Each rider's time for each stage is recorded and the overall winner is the one with the lowest total. The greatest stage race is also the most famous cycling event in the world, the Tour de France. The professional cyclists who ride this grueling contest average more than 100 miles a day for almost a month, and they go through the most demanding terrain the promoters can find in the Alps and Pyrenees.

The physical requirements of bicycle road racing are nowhere more vividly portrayed than when compared to marathon running. A world-class marathoner will cover the 26.2 miles in under 2 hours and 12 minutes. It is such a brutal test that Olympic champion Frank Shorter says it takes him a month to recover. No one could ever run marathons on two or more consecutive days and hope to be competitive. Yet a 100-mile bike race takes about four hours and world-class cyclists are able to handle that effort daily for two weeks or more.

Added to the sheer magnitude of the cyclist's mileage is the nature of the bike itself. A runner has to carry his own weight and when he becomes exhausted he must walk or stop. The cyclist, however, is supported by the bike and this frees all his energy for forward motion. When he becomes fatigued he can recover on downhills or in the wind shelter of the pack. In this way he can drive himself into exhaustion and then recoup his strength for another such effort several times during a race.

Because of such physical demands, bike racers are among the world's most fit people. We regularly register the highest oxygen uptake values of any athletes, challenged only by fellow masochists like cross-country skiers and long-distance runners and swimmers. The aforementioned Bob Cook had an oxygen uptake value approaching twice that of athletes in more sedentary sports like football.

Cyclists' hearts have adapted to the strain by developing the ability to pump much more blood per beat than normal hearts. As a result they don't need to beat as often, giving bike racers phenomenally low resting pulses. A figure of 32 to 40 beats per minute is not uncommon, and this has led to some strange confrontations with doctors who have dealt with sick people so long that they don't know what to do with super healthy ones.

As an example, several years ago a racer of my acquaintance was hit by a car while on a training ride. Although his injuries were minor he was taken to the emergency room for observation. A physician swabbed out the scrapes and was ready to release him until the nurse handed over the blood pressure and pulse readings. Both were nearly normal for this particular rider (105/60 and 42), but the doctor was convinced that his patient was suffering from shock and he ordered him hospitalized. It took two days for the racer to convince the medical staff that he was not at death's door.

And, of course, there are the crashes. The bicycle is by nature an unstable beast and it tends to obey the laws of gravity. Crashes are so much a part of the sport that dedicated riders will simply ignore the clash of skin and blacktop and scramble back on to finish the race. The most common malady is called "road rash," the livid result of tender epidermis skidding along the concrete at 30 miles per hour.

Crashes damage expensive equipment, too, and more than one cyclist has purposely taken the impact on his legs or back rather than scratch up a new Masi or Colnago. Referring to the outrageously expensive but *de rigueur* Italian components, one sage and scarred Veteran put it succinctly: "Flesh heals; Campagnolo doesn't."

It is possible to get irrevocably hooked on bicycle racing with less than world-class doses. As I write this at age 35 I am ancient by American athletic standards and handicapped by a lack of time to train. In a sport where the weekly mileage of national-level athletes hovers around 400 and top riders do little but eat, sleep and ride, I have to fit my training around my profession and family. From March to June this means riding through the cold and gloom at 5 a.m. But I don't consider myself ill-used. John Allis, who won a National Road Championship at the age of 32, was a hospital administrator at the time and trained at 4 a.m.

Like a true addict, I have become thin and drawn. When I graduated from high school I was a wiry 155 pounds and had a football scholarship clutched in my adolescent hand. I quickly found that survival on the gridiron at that weight was impossible, so I devoted myself to growing. Aided by dedicated weight training and conscientious overeating, I played college ball at 205. By the time I finished my career I had fallen victim to a syndrome in American sports which equates manhood with physical size.

At 205 pounds I looked like a beer barrel on skids, but I was so afraid of getting skinny that I continued to eat like Rosey Grier. It was to no avail. The artificially trained-on bulk vanished as my overactive metabolism consumed the excess. To my mortification my shirt size dwindled from 17 to 15. Then, after three years of training on the bike, I was back to a lean 150 pounds.

Dr. Ken Cooper and other gurus of fitness would say I am now at a much healthier weight than during my football days, though sometimes I am not so sure. Friends who used to tell me I look like I had caused a famine now say I resemble the victim. Because of my continuous weight loss, a minor fortune in outsized clothes hangs in my closet.

With virtually no excess fat to provide reserves, I fuel my training and regular daily activities solely with what I consume meal by meal. A missed breakfast, lunch or dinner is a catastrophe. Unless I eat continually on long rides I fall victim to the dreaded "bonk," a weakened condition that causes the sufferer to pedal in lumpy squares and see big black spots in front of his eyes. Somewhere there is a balance between emaciation and ponderousness, but I suspect I missed it both going up and coming down.

Then there is the matter of my cardiovascular system. Racing has reduced my resting pulse to less than 40. According to the experts I should be immune from heart attacks and related diseases. Surely that is a positive benefit. Yet when I stand abruptly I get so dizzy that I have to bend over until the blood returns to my poor abused brain cells. This is perfectly normal, according to the experts, who say that exercise-induced low blood pressure is a sign that I am in superior condition. Superior, perhaps, but also potentially embarrassing. I live in fear of the day when I will collapse ignominiously in my classroom as I rise to write on the board, or when I pitch headlong into the *hors d'oeuvres* at a social gathering.

So what is an outwardly sane adult with a responsible profession, a lovely wife and an adoring son doing in a sport like this? I have often wondered that myself while on a 100-mile training ride, which provides many purgatorial hours to contemplate such questions. Even with all the time spent pondering, though, I haven't been able to come up with anything definite.

But I suspect that it has something to do with shameless pride, with knowing that I am more fit than most other people on earth.

I think it has a little to do with ambition. I am fascinated by my own improvement and addicted to the "high" that a better performance brings.

I know that it has to do with emotional release. The stress and frustration of the day dissolve at a heart rate of 150-plus, and a hard jam up a hill blows away everything but the elemental me.

It certainly is a function of competition. I am always amazed at the reserves I have left when I really want to beat someone else.

But most of all, my addiction is life-giving and life-enhancing. When I race or ride hard I feel my existence in every nerve and muscle fiber, from burning lungs to aching legs. My training rides get me out in the sun and wind and make my senses more alert than during the rest of the day. Solutions to previously insurmountable problems and ways to express what had been only a feeling have come more easily during a ride. Racing itself reveals physical and psychological limits that the sedentary soul never sees.

I admit unashamedly that cycling is pure fun, play. Something of the unconscious exhilaration of the child or animal is released in the speed of downhills and the gravity-defying sweep of cornering. It helps put the seemingly grave problems of each day into a more realistic perspective.

I suspect that my addiction is positive after all. And as addicts are wont to do, my intention is to help you sample this pleasure — the experience of fast riding for fitness and competition — that satisfies me so.

Do you train to race or race to train? Some riders like the motivation of occasional competition to give some purpose to their conditioning program. Others race simply because they love competition. Whatever your motivation, serious cycling can change your habits for eating, exercise and personal conduct, leading to what some call the fitness lifestyle.

2
Entering
the Unknown
Apprehensive first steps may lead
to a lifetime of health and vigor

THIS BOOK IS designed for two groups of riders. It is for the beginning cyclist of any age or sex — the person who has never used a bike seriously for either physical fitness or competition but now wants to, though unsure about how to get started. It is also for the more experienced rider who is excited about racing and personal improvement yet who must find the time and techniques to fit training around a job, school and/or family. Let's look at these truly amateur athletes more closely.

Some like the motivation of occasional competition to sustain and nourish their personal conditioning program. They are often fine riders who are strongest in solitary events like time trials, but they may not race frequently. As one such rider commented, "I don't race much because it disrupts my training schedule." These cyclists tend to mix other activities like touring, long one-day rides, running, cross-country skiing and backpacking into their overall athletic programs. Although riding and racing are important to them, their primary goal is development and maintenance of the fitness necessary to lead active and exciting lives.

Other riders race because they love competition. Many of these are older men and women who were athletes in school and have found cycling to be a perfect outlet for their competitive instincts. These riders tend to have aggressive personalities and the danger is that they will attack cycling as they do most activities, trying, to get too good too fast. They can fall prey to overtraining injuries or the loss of interest that occurs when they can't achieve the often unrealistic goals they set for themselves.

And some people race, I suspect, out of a sense of positive elitism. The roads are full of runners these days, but serious cyclists — much less licensed racers, of which there were about

23,000 in the U.S. in 1986 — are a relatively rare breed. In the very obscurity of the sport lies much of its fascination and attraction to the free spirit.

But regardless of their motivation, serious riders often adopt (sometimes unconsciously) what might be called the fitness life-style. Out of a cycling avocation arise habits for eating, exercise and personal conduct that not only produce a better racer but also promote the important by-products of health, vigor and en-thusiasm for life.

If you fit any of these descriptions, or would like to, I invite you to make the sport of cycling yours. In following chapters I will explore topics like training principles and techniques, time bud-geting, equipment, racing skills, nutrition and everything else that should help you get maximum benefit from your riding.

Beginnings are always frightening, involved as they are with the unknown. The prospect of entering the world of competitive cycling is perhaps fraught with more anxiety than most other ventures. Many people have begun to run road races but relatively few compete in bike races. Why is this? Expense and the formality of getting a U.S. Cycling Federation license have something to do with it, as does the relative scarcity of cycling events. However, I think the main reason is the apprehension that afflicts prospective racers. This can easily be overcome with a little experience, practice and knowledge, so I will be mentioning ways to alleviate or lessen the physical and mental resistances to racing that almost every beginner feels.

One of the important factors in gaining confidence as a rider is feeling safe on the bike, and towards that end a good helmet is essential. Forget everything you ever heard about hardshell helmets being hot; ignore the stares, real or imagined, of non-cyclists; and most of all ignore the traditionalists who disdain any head protection for training and wear helmets in races only because the rules require it. Get a quality hardshell helmet made for cycling and wear it every time you get on the bike. The roads are full of hazards. As a new racer you will probably be riding faster in training than you are used to, which can lead to bike-handling errors and crashes. Cars are an ever-present danger. Senior III-IV races sometimes have a disproportionate number of casualties caused when the heat of competition combines with fatigue to breed poor judgment. In any of these situations you need all the head protection you can get, and having it will take a big load off your mind.

An upcoming chapter deals with all the clothing and equipment you need for training and racing (and how to save money obtaining it), but the helmet can't wait. Make it your first priority if you haven't already. In races sanctioned by the U.S. Cycling Federation you must wear a helmet which meets or exceeds Snell Memorial or ANSI Z-90.4 standards. Hardshells manufactured Bell, Monarch, Vetta and other companies which meet these standards have all won devoted wearers and saved lives. Check them out and buy the one that fits you correctly and comfortably.

There is another prerequisite to beginning the kind of strenuous exertion that training and racing demand: a complete physical checkup. This is especially important if you are over 30 and have led a relatively sedentary life for several years. Even those who golf, play tennis on weekends, jog occasionally, etc. are included — none of these activities is sufficient conditioning for what you are about to undertake. To make sure you will not ride your bike into health problems instead of health benefits, see your doctor, discuss the training methods this book outlines and get his go-ahead. If you have been riding 25 miles several times a week or running about 30 miles a week you probably have an adequate base from which to begin more stressful workouts. Still, a physical exam is recommended if you haven't had one in recent years.

Figuring your proper frame size

Position on the bike is very important for any kind of cycling but especially for racing. In order to get the most out of your physical ability two criteria must be met: (1) the frame must be the appropriate size for your body; (2) you must sit on the bike in a position that allows you to pedal correctly in biomechanical terms and also handle the bike with ease and precision. Unfortunately, there is no consensus on exactly what constitutes the ideal for either of the above; perhaps there can never be, given the limitless variation in human physiques (and reasoning). What is certain is that you must step back and take care of these two essentials before beginning or expanding your cycling program.

When it comes to frame size many riders seem to equate bigger with better. Actually, the opposite is true, especially when dealing with racing bikes. As English framebuilder Dave Moulton has written in *Velo-news*, "One advantage of a small frame is very obvious: It is lighter. But more importantly, the tubes are shorter and that means the frame is more rigid and responsive. When you ride a smaller bike you sit over it and dominate it, you can handle it better and put it where you want it. On the other hand, riding a big frame is like sitting astride a field gate.''

Moulton doesn't suggest that you can't be on a frame that is too small, but he notes that American cyclists in particular are caught up in what has been called the big-frame syndrome. Are you a victim, wittingly or otherwise? Find out by sitting on your bike with the crank arms horizontal to the ground and see if you can squeeze the top tube between your knees. If so, fine. But if your knees touch below the tube then it is a pretty good indication that the frame is larger than you need. You can make adjustments to achieve a reasonable riding position and the bike will be satisfactory for fitness cycling, but it may be a limiting factor as you strive to improve in racing.

If you will be purchasing a new or used frame or bike, Moulton gives a simple formula for determining what should be the best frame size for competitive cycling: two-thirds of the rider's inseam length, measured from crotch to floor without shoes. The resulting figure should equal the frame size, measured from the center of the crank axle to the top of the seat tube. For example, a rider with a 36-inch inseam should have a 24-inch frame while one with a 30-inch inseam should ride a 20-inch frame. Moulton cautions that riders with exceptionally long feet should increase the frame size an inch or so; those with small feet for their leg length should go slightly smaller than the formula says.

Finding your best riding position

Once a bike of appropriate size is under you, there is the all-important matter of determining your optimum riding position. Two oft-cited methods are useful but not the last word. The first is to visit your local bike shop or club and enlist the aid of an experienced cyclist or coach. He can observe your body dimensions and riding style to help make the necessary adjustments to the saddle and handlebars. This works best if the person you pick doesn't have an unusual style himself. The other way is to study the pictures of top road riders and emulate their positions. Be careful to choose those who have a physical structure similar to yours.

If a bike shop near you has a sizing device such as the Fit Kit or the Serotta Size-Cycle, it is worth the reasonable fee to take advantage of this service. These ingenious tools can help you in selecting the right size bike and also in setting up your position. Using the Fit Kit, shop personnel take several measurements on you, then use charts to determine your best frame size, stem and top tube combination, handlebar width, and crank size. Measurements of hundreds of top riders serve as the basis of the figures on the charts. The Size-Cycle is an adjustable bicycle frame. By sitting on it you can experiment with different frame sizes, saddle positions, and stem lengths.

If you would prefer to do it yourself by the numbers, here is a step-by-step method for adjusting the bike to accommodate your personal dimensions. It is taken in part from *Cycling*, the authoritative publication of Italy's Central Sports School.

1. Loosen the seat post clamp sufficiently to slide the saddle fore and aft. Sit on the bike in your normal riding position. Someone can hold you up, or you can do this next to a wall or with your bike mounted on a Racer-Mate or similar stand. Find the bony protuberance just below your knee at the top of the shin. With the crank arm forward and parallel to the floor, a plumb line dropped from that bump should be directly over the pedal axle. Have someone observe your normal foot position through that point in the pedal stroke, then hold your foot at that same angle (if any) while you make this check. Move the saddle fore or aft to achieve the correct position.

2. Before tightening the clamp, set the tilt of the saddle in relation to the bike. To see this clearly you should place a yardstick or broom handle along the center line of the saddle from back to front and note the angle it makes to the frame's top tube. Make the saddle parallel to the tube or slightly nose up, depending on your preference, but never nose down — you will tend to slide forward, putting strain on the arms and shoulders. Tighten the saddle and post as one.

3. Now determine the saddle height that will help you achieve correct pedal action and efficient application of power. Get into your riding shorts and cycling shoes, set the bike near a wall and sit squarely on the saddle. Put your heels on the pedals, using the wrong sides if toe clips and straps are in place. When pedaling backwards from this position your knees should straighten as the pedals reach their lowest position, but there must be no swaying of the buttocks in order for the heels to keep contact. Adjust the height of the saddle accordingly. It is best for road riders to have a saddle slightly on the low side rather than too high.

4. Turning to the handlebars, they should be positioned so that the drops are parallel to the ground or angled slightly forward. The top of the stem should always be lower than the top of the saddle, though how much is limited by the need to see and breathe

Former world champion Marianne Berglund, at 5-foot-4 and 110 pounds, is an example of the fact that small size and light weight can be a successful formula for road racing.

At 6-foot-2 and 150 pounds Olympic gold medalist Alexi Grewal has the thin, wiry build considered essential for success in climbing and stage racing. In his native Colorado he holds the record for the Mt. Evans Hill Climb and has won the mountainous Morgul-Bismarck stage of the Coors Classic.

Jeff Pierce's curved back violates the flat, sleek profile most coaches want to see. But this "imperfection" has not prevented him from becoming one of the best U.S. stage racers. Pierce has finished in the top 10 overall at the Coors Classic three times.

without hindrance. If the stem is too high you will have too much weight on the saddle; if too low you won't be comfortable or efficient when riding on the drops, the primary racing position. You are looking for a weight distribution of about 45% on the front wheel and 55% on the rear. Most riders will find that placing the stem about 5-7 centimeters below saddle height will produce both a comfortable and aerodynamic position.

   5. The final factor is stem extension. Climb back on the bike and assume a position with your hands on the drops just as if you were riding. Now look at your front hub. If you can't see it because the handlebars are in your line of vision, or if it appears just behind the bars, the extension is fine. If, however, you see the hub in front of the bars it is a good indication that your upper body will be too upright and cramped for efficient riding. Also, the bike won't handle as crisply as it should. Calculate the stem extension needed to bring you into the ballpark and visit your local dealer or club. Sometimes there will be used stems available because others needed to do just what you are up to now.

   One other variable is toe clip length. There are three sizes (small, medium, large) and the correct choice is the one that will position the ball of your foot over the pedal axle. Remember that the shoe doesn't fit fully into the end of the clip; a small space is needed to prevent pressure on your toes and allow the cleat to engage and disengage easily. If you have the new Look pedals or some other strapless model, follow the same rule: The ball of your foot should be over the pedal axle.

   My recommendation is to use all the various techniques — advice, imitation, formulation — to establish your approximate frame size and basic riding position, then settle on what feels and works best. A little experimentation is something every rider tries, especially in the beginning. Just remember to make position changes one at a time in small increments, giving each a few rides to settle in. In this way you will be able to accurately assess the results, and you will diminish the risk of muscle and joint problems that can occur with wild fluctuations in the bike setup. I firmly believe that any physiological study of saddle height and all the sage advice of a coach is worthless if individual differences and quirks aren't allowed for, so go ahead and make intelligent alterations.

Apprehension

   Physical concerns such as frame size and riding position are only part of what causes uncertainty for the aspiring competitor.

When he considers actually entering his first race, perhaps the most important resistances are psychological. It is my contention that the value of any new experience is often directly proportional to the fear and anxiety felt while considering it. If this is so, bike racing rates a high mark.

Many potential bike racers never try to compete because they are afraid they can't hold the pace. First on the list of a beginner's fears is the vision of being spit out the back of a Senior IV pack while spectators and other racers look on in faintly concealed derision. Although it is difficult to find out if you can keep up in a race without actually giving it a try, there are some ways to estimate your ability. They can help your confidence and reduce the unknown a little.

The best way is to train with other racers. They will give you an honest, sometimes brutal, sizing up. But perhaps you are isolated from experienced competitors. In this case you can ride time trials on a flat course and compare results with those for your District's 40-kilometer USCF championship. Keep in mind, however, that the District times represent the best in the area. As a beginner you will usually be riding against people with considerably less horsepower. Also, wind, terrain and motivation are factors that can affect performances in any given event.

Some people never race because they are afraid of crashing. Few specters frighten the beginning rider as much as that of skin and bone sliding across the macadam. Even athletes who are used to contact and falls — football and hockey players or skiers, for instance — recoil in horror at the thought of their tender epidermis left in strips on the road. It is true that accidents seem to be more numerous during the first year or so of serious riding. However, most crashes involve only superficial abrasions and an occasional shoulder/collarbone injury. The major exception is the possibility of head wounds, which underscores the importance of a good hard helmet for protection and for increasing confidence.

Crashes, like floor burns in basketball or sore knees in running, are just part of the sport. The seasoned competitor does everything in his power to avoid falling but doesn't waste energy worrying about the possibility.

Above all, the prospective racer must realize that at some point he just has to begin. Like the first time you went off the high board, there is no substitute for wheeling your bike to the starting line and taking the plunge. You won't be sorry you tried it, but don't be discouraged if the initial result is as poor as you feared.

As we'll see, it takes time to develop muscular endurance and cardiovascular capacity, to say nothing of race strategy, riding skills and mental toughness. In bike racing as in other endeavors, experience and persistence pay big dividends.

3
Determination

*A strong will to succeed
can minimize physical limitations*

WHEN I AM not riding or writing, I make a living teaching literature and composition. The most enjoyable aspect of this profession is the opportunity to discuss ideas arising from the works we study. It is an intellectually exciting daily routine, especially when I find concepts that can be applied to cycling.

For instance, in the process of studying *Oedipus Rex* and *Paradise Lost* we discussed the concept of predestination and free will: To what extent are we able to control our own futures, make our own choices and generally act like autonomous individuals? Can we choose what we will be, or are our ultimate achievements influenced by genetic and environmental factors over which we have no control?

Judging from bike racers' concerns, this subject is of practical as well as philosophical interest. They ask: Can the factors that limit performance on the bike be overcome by one's will and determination? Allow me to speculate on this crucial question, citing physiological studies as well as personal experience.

In general, it appears that an individual's upper limits of performance are genetically fixed. There are numerous stories of racers who have trained relatively little and yet done well on pure inherited ability. Two examples are Tom Doughty's sub 57-minute time trial with no training between races, and John Patterson's Junior National TT Championship which came on his first attempt at the event.

On the other hand, few racers approach their upper limits. It is conventional wisdom that a moderately talented rider who works hard can defeat the genetically blessed but less committed competitor. If you assume that natural talent determines 75% of performance and that mental attitude coupled with training accounts for the remaining 25%, the odds are overwhelmingly against the modestly talented rider. Yet you can do a tremendous amount of improving within the limits of that 25%.

But hard work is not all the answer; nothing is as simple as it seems. The less-gifted rider may also be only moderately talented in the ability to recover. His resolve to train hard could make him more susceptible to overtraining and result in exhaustion and lessened performance rather than improvement. The rich get richer while the poor get saddle sores, tendon problems and chronic fatigue.

Thus, talent and hard work are only two-thirds of the equation. Also important is determining how much training makes you improve and at what point you break down. This sort of wisdom comes only through patience, experience and careful observation.

As a specific example, consider the ability to sprint. Obviously, you can accelerate either by turning the cranks faster or by using a bigger gear. However, employing a big gear does not often make for a very effective sprint. This is because acceleration time is lengthened even though top speed may be relatively great. A racer without the ability to jump quickly to top speed will win very few sprints.

To improve sprinting ability a rider needs to be able to attain a high cadence. Yet research indicates that leg speed and reaction time are related to the proportion of fast- and slow-twitch fibers in muscles. Scientists further believe that this fiber mix is genetically determined. You can do things to improve your sprint, but if you have a large percentage of slow-twitch fibers you will usually be beaten in short efforts by a rider more favorably endowed, regardless of how much you practice.

To make this genetic lottery seem even more unfair, consider this: The rider with a high percentage of slow-twitch fibers should have superior endurance and thus be able to hammer his opponents into submission in the miles leading up to the finish. Unfortunately, it appears that slow-twitch muscle fibers can't have their efficiency improved for sprinting as much as endurance can be improved in fast-twitch fibers. So the sprinter has a better chance of hanging in and accelerating effectively than the stayer does of grinding down his faster opponents. However, the outcome of a race depends so much on tactics and other variables that sheer physical ability is often transcended. Most results cannot be predicted by a muscle biopsy.

Exercise physiologists themselves have difficulty interpreting their experiments. Many studies on fast- and slow-twitch muscle fiber have been done on established competitors who have spent years training for either speed or endurance. Couldn't their muscle fiber make-ups be due in part to their bodies' adaptation to training? The results of these studies seem only to reveal a riddle: Does the activity make your muscles adapt, or do you choose the activity to which you are most adapted?

Another example of the cloudy relationship between performance and talent is percent of body fat. Some people have systems that store fat easily. This is unfortunate in our weight-conscious society and it makes endurance sports more difficult, but biologically it is extremely useful because the stored fat provides emergency fuel and reserves.

Can the naturally bulky individual attain the leanness necessary for top performance? Perhaps, but mere miles usually won't make it happen. He also has to limit food intake and this can lead to loss of strength. Some naturally lean racers can eat prodigiously, and they have to in order to sustain the energy needed to ride hard without sacrificing their power-to-weight ratio. On the other hand, the mesomorphic cyclist can train intensely for shorter periods and be potentially stronger because of his more rugged, muscular constitution.

I suspect that some riders cannot get below a certain percent of body fat without seriously compromising health and performance, while others can maintain an incredible leanness and still retain strength and vigor. For them body fat levels of 5% and below are perfectly feasible, perhaps even their physiological norm. Others go to pieces when they sink below 8-10%. They may diet in an attempt to get closer to "ideal" levels and succeed only in losing strength.

A case in point is a fit rider of my acquaintance who registered 9.5% fat at a body weight of 168. He set up a sensible diet program and gradually lost 20 pounds in 14 months. Yet at 148 his body fat had only dropped to 8.5%. In spite of the long-term combination of diet and exercise, most of his weight loss was muscle tissue. It showed in his lessened ability to turn big gears and his decreased energy for training and other everyday activities.

Apparently this rider's body, for its own protection, refused to allow the fat percentage to sink below a certain genetically determined level. When food intake was reduced, the body metabolized protein instead of fat. Solution? The rider could eat more and gain a dozen pounds, but it isn't that simple. If he merely eats and rides, the calories in excess of energy needs will be converted to fat and he would be in danger of weighing 160 pounds with 10% fat. He would have less muscle, more fat and less success than he had at 168 before devoting so much time and will power to

Sean Kelly, winner of numerous European classics, is often cited as an example of what can be accomplished with a strong innner drive. In 1986 a leg injury kept him out of the Tour de France but he came back strong late in the season and won the Super Prestige Trophy for best professional for the third year in a row.

improvement. He needs to eat more, ride and also lift weights to restore the muscle/fat ratio that is optimum for his personal physiology.

Although the research of exercise physiologists has been useful and interesting, it cannot be perceived as a substitute for pure common sense and intuitive knowledge of one's own body. Studies may show the body fat of elite cyclists to be a certain percent, but this doesn't mean that the beginning racer should ignore all other factors in order to get to that level. Maybe you will never be able to perform as well as the more gifted athlete regardless of how hard you work. However, you can strive for your maximum potential within your own genetic range and shoot for personal goals. And when you seek your limits you'll likely find some surprises.

I believe that the rider of limited potential who takes maximum advantage of his ability — who loves the sport, plans his workouts wisely, and painfully wrests training time from the demands of everyday life — may have a deeper appreciation and a more complete grasp of the competitive experience than a rider whose talent is greater but whose commitment is less. Real champions, of course, have both natural talent and the desire to work hard. It is the blending of these two factors — physical and mental — that makes sport the challenge that it is.

I hope the day never comes when doctors can test each 6-year-old and predict his maximum in every endeavor. My experience in sports, as well as my undeniable prejudice, affirms that the resources of the human will defy all categorization.

4
Making Do

*Imperfect cycling situations
needn't thwart your development*

MOST TRAINING AND RACING advice seems based on the assumption that we live in the best of all possible cycling worlds. It is taken for granted that we have other cyclists nearby for training partners, access to Nautilus machines and exercise physiologists, a plethora of local races or a major USCF event within easy reach each weekend, and several pro bike shops just around the corner.

I don't have any of these things, and I suspect that the majority of U.S. racing cyclists also can be classified as "disadvantaged" in the sense that most of the optimum conditions for growth and development don't exist in the immediate environment. Still, it's true that in order for a beginning racer to really improve he needs certain advantages to nurture inborn talent. Like a culturally or emotionally deprived child, a novice racer will not grow and develop as much in a sterile atmosphere as when all sorts of cycling stimulation are available.

The ideal environment for the beginning racer includes easily accessible roads with flat to rolling terrain (and some severe climbs) within a 50-mile radius. The climate should be moderate much of the year, although a little wintry weather for several months could be an advantage in that it requires getting off the bike and into some other activity like running or cross-country skiing. This respite is advantageous mentally as well as physically.

The perfect environment would also include other riders of all abilities. The obvious advantage is in having a pool of potential training partners and a nucleus of racers for local and club events, but there is also a less obvious benefit: The more cyclists on the road, the more accustomed local motorists become to the sight of bike riders. Theoretically, the roads will be safer.

A local pro bike shop is useful both for immediate access to parts and advice and for some repairs that are impractical in the home workshop. Often it is the dealer of quality equipment who will help organize and sponsor a local cycling club.

The most important criterion is a good schedule of nearby races. And it helps if the cyclist's immediate environment includes money because equipment and travel for racing can be expensive.

Not many of the approximately 23,000 USCF-licensed competitors have all of these optimum conditions. If you don't, either, and are not young, independent, totally dedicated to the sport and eager to relocate to some ideal place, you will have to do the best with what you have. Fortunately, there are ways to overcome most of what is lacking.

The lone trainer

What if you live where there are no other racing cyclists nearby? I am one of two licensed riders in a 70-mile radius, so I empathize with the problem. If you are in a similar situation you will need to make some modifications in your training if you hope to be competitive.

Be sure to include at least one LSD outing per week even if you hate long solo rides. LSD is more fun with company, but by yourself you can go at an optimum pace and you won't get slowed down by other riders' problems. You also must include intervals and speed work in your training when the natural intensity of group rides is absent. I find that when I train alone I tend to fall into the habit of grinding steadily away, a training technique that may be useful for time trials but does little to accustom me to the constant pace changes of road racing.

Bike handling is the lone trainer's biggest problem — you just don't get used to having the distraction and danger of other bikes around. To increase your familiarity with how your own bike handles, you can try a little cyclocross or dress in heavy sweats, put on old wheels and do all sorts of daredevil maneuvers on a grass surface. Unfortunately, most of your group riding practice will be in the races themselves, which is not so good for you or the riders around you. Even simple things like making smooth gear changes can become difficult in the commotion of a pack when you're not used to having such activity just inches away. I suppose that riding in heavy traffic is good practice, but the penalties for a mistake are so grave that I hesitate to recommend it.

The problem of money is not so insurmountable. Although it would help to be able to buy unlimited cycling equipment, the sport can be pursued with a surprisingly modest investment, as I discuss in another chapter. In general, fancy and expensive equipment, clothes and components don't make you that much better. Too many beginners blame poor results on what they consider to be inferior equipment, but that is almost never the reason.

Should you live in an area where there is no pro bike shop nearby, it's possible to buy your cycling needs through the mail. There has been a controversy over discount prices offered by mailorder suppliers versus greater service at the local shop, but it doesn't matter if there isn't a shop to patronize.

Sharing the road

Some riders face a tough situation because motorists don't give them any respect. I used to think this was a matter of location, that conservative rural areas had a larger percentage of potential troublemakers than more cosmopolitan urban environments. That stereotype has dissolved with my experiences of the last several years. I live in a small farming and ranching town, replete with pickups sporting guns in the back window, cowboys both real and pseudo, and a highly visible minority of citizens whose idea of vigorous exercise is to drive up into the mountains and then tear up the tundra with their dirt bikes. However, I have never been seriously challenged, threatened or even insulted in 13 years of training on the roads we all share.

Yet across state in the sophisticated atmosphere of Boulder, whose residents have been annually exposed to top-flight racing by the Coors Classic, I spent a miserable eight weeks while doing graduate work at the University of Colorado. I had to train in unbearable traffic among frustrated and belligerent drivers, plus several truckers who can only be described as homicidal maniacs. But I shouldn't gloat about the safety of my home turf. It only takes one careless, aggressive or inebriated driver to remind me that stereotypes breed a false sense of security and that every day on the road is a new risk.

You can reduce the danger from hostile humans by riding legally and maintaining a low profile. Don't draw attention to yourself by dangerous or showy antics or sudden moves in traffic. Wear bright colors so drowsy motorists can see you. When hassled, try to get a license number and description. Write letters to the editor of the community paper bemoaning the dangers of local roads. If that doesn't help, perhaps an educational article or two aimed at drivers and sanctioned by the local police department or state patrol will work.

Above all, don't get paranoid. Most drivers aren't really out to get you, although some days it seems like it.

Racing opportunities

Probably the biggest disadvantage for the aspiring racer comes if you live far from races. Runners can compete infrequently and still do well because most foot races are basically time trials and don't require special skills or tactics. A cyclist, however, needs to race in order to become and stay competitive.

I have partially solved the problem by picking my races carefully. In April I usually drive the 600-mile round trip to the Denver area, where most Colorado races are held, for my first event of the season. We get a babysitter and I take my wife for a weekend in the big city; I treat the race as an important by-product. I make sure to check the weather carefully because nothing is more frustrating than driving six hours across the state on Friday night only to wake on race day to snow, sleet and cancellation. Also, I call ahead to be sure that the race is actually going to happen; club schedules are often more an expression of hopes than a guarantee.

If I can get in that one race in April I feel fortunate. In May there are two "local" events — 70 and 110 miles away — which I try to hit. Then in the middle of June it's back to Denver for the USCF District Championships. The rest of the summer I play it week by week. I have raced from five to 15 times annually in the past 12 years, but the big total was when I was in Boulder for the summer. These numbers are far from ideal, but you have to work within the limitations of your situation.

Other solutions: Begin your own unsanctioned local time trial series; ride several carefully chosen races every year and try to peak for each; supplement your limited racing with long one-day rides — you can get in some excellent base miles and have a challenge, too, if you see how far you can ride on raceless weekends; push yourself on tours of one or several days; specialize in time trials that don't require race experience or pack riding skills.

The obvious solution to all the above disadvantages would be to move to that ideal location having the best blend of factors for racing development. However, most of us aren't able or willing to make that commitment to the sport. Like many cyclists, I have chosen where I live because of factors unrelated to competition — in my case because of that elusive something called quality of life. Montrose may be far removed from the mainstream of U.S. bike racing, but it is a great place to live and has ideal cycling conditions.

If you are alert to the possibilities, nearly any shortcoming can be negated or even turned into a positive factor. When it comes down to it, you are a disadvantaged cyclist only if you allow yourself to be.

5
Wheels
for the Runner
Cycling offers much for those
injured or frustrated by running

IF YOU COUNT YOURSELF among the estimated 30 million Americans who run regularly, you may have never seriously considered cycling as an alternate sport or a means to improving your performance. But don't go away — as a person who competes on feet as well as on wheels, I know the sports are compatible and even mutually beneficial. A runner who doesn't include cycling in the arsenal of training techniques is missing (1) a valuable aid to racing fitness and (2) a therapeutic tool. And if you are a competitive runner who is dissatisfied with race performances, you may even find cycling to be your best sport.

Running and cycling have long been considered incompatible sports, cyclocross notwithstanding. Even worse, a certain amount of barely concealed hostility has existed between the two groups, runners reveling in the popularity explosion of their sport while cyclists cite bike racing's exclusive circle of participants and "hard man" reputation. In a case of mass popularity versus snob appeal, both groups have been guilty of unfounded and self-defeating prejudice. For instance, Dr. Joan Ullyot, in her book *Running Free*, discusses the aerobic activities which injured runners can do to maintain fitness. She includes bike riding but comments that "cyclists are a group apart . . . cyclists would rather be cycling and runners would rather be running."

On the other hand, *Bicycling* magazine once ran a cover article entitled "Beating Runners at Their Own Game." The tone of the piece was tongue-in-cheek, but the outraged response revealed the depth of the misunderstanding among participants in the two sports.

It may come as a surprise, then, that a number of quality athletes have discovered the affinities between running and cy-

Inga Benedict was a competitive runner before taking up cycling and making the 1984 Olympic team. For her — as for many others — the switch was motivated by running injuries.

cling. Veteran New Zealand marathoner Jack Foster, who ran a 2:14 after he had turned 40, started his competitive career as a bike racer. His usual training day after he switched to running consisted of a commute to work on his bike as well as a 10-mile run. 7-Eleven star Inga Benedict was a competitive runner before injuries forced her into cycling. A year later she made the Olympic cycling squad. The man often called the "cyclist of the decade" of the '70s, John Howard, ran competitively in high school and demonstrated that running and cycling do indeed mix well when he won the 1981 Ironman Triathlon in Hawaii, in which both disciplines plus swimming are featured. Ex-runner Mike Engleman shocked the California racing commmunity with his hillclimbing ability during the 1986 season. In addition, hundreds of other athletes combine running and cycling with success, enjoyment and deep satisfaction.

Let's clear up some of the misconceptions that may be keeping you, the runner, off the bike.

The facts about cycling

One is the mistaken idea, held by many runners and fostered at times by running magazines, that you can't get fit by cycling. You can't get your heart rate high enough, detractors say, because it is too easy to coast down hills and because the bike supports your body weight. That this is not true was amply demonstrated by a running friend of mine who was forced to ride for six weeks while a marathon injury healed. He saw the layoff as a disaster to his fitness and future racing hopes. He complained bitterly that when riding he couldn't work hard enough to induce the training effect.

I questioned him and found that his bike had no toe clips and straps. Further, he was plodding along in his biggest gear at 60 pedal revolutions per minute because he believed that the bigger the gear, the more exercise he was getting. I installed clips and straps for him, got him to select a smaller gear, and then we went for a ride at a brisk 100 cadence. Judging from the sound of heavy breathing behind me, I knew his beliefs about the quality of cycling workouts were rapidly being altered. Far from being a poor way to increase cardiovascular capacity, bike riding has enormous advantages for the person who seeks optimum fitness.

Another criticism is that it takes too long to get a good workout on the bike. You have to ride for an hour or longer, I've heard it said, to get the benefits equal to 30 minutes of running. This isn't true. Any two activities that elevate the heart rate to the same level for an equivalent amount of time are equally beneficial to the cardiovascular system. It doesn't matter if you run for 30 minutes at a heart rate of 140 or ride for 30 at 140 — you receive the same amount of cardiovascular stimulation. Those who say they can't get a workout on the bike just aren't spinning their legs fast enough. Also, cycling specifically uses the quadriceps muscles while running's stress is more spread out. As a result, a cyclist feels more localized fatigue than a runner when both are working at the same heart rate, at least in the first experiences. Because of this, runners often feel as though they are working much harder on the bike for fewer results. Once their quadriceps adapt, it's no longer a problem.

Detractors of cycling are also heard to say that it is an inefficient way to burn calories. For proof they cite studies showing that running consumes about 100 calories per mile while cycling's caloric cost is only about 40 per mile. What they neglect is the fact that you go faster on the bike, covering more miles in a given period of time. Hence, you will burn about the same number of calories per hour in either activity. For instance, a 150-pound man running at a pace of around 7:30 per mile will use about 800 calories in an hour. In that same period, a reasonably fit cyclist can cover 20 miles and, at 40 calories per mile, will also use about 800. So cycling is just as efficient a consumer of excess body fat as running when the two activities are compared on a time basis.

In fact, in one way cycling is far superior to running in this regard. Studies have shown that the best method of reducing one's percent of body fat is to train long and relatively slowly. At such an aerobic pace the body will burn fat, whereas anaerobic activity is powered solely by glycogen. During aerobic exercise lasting two hours or more, the body will begin to substantially use fat stores for fuel. However, it is difficult for most runners to exercise for that length of time on a consistent basis. Many have the aerobic capacity to run for several hours, but the weight-bearing nature of the sport practically guarantees some sort of tendon, knee or foot problem from continued long runs.

Cycling, because it is not a weight-bearing activity and because it involves a smooth, non-jarring motion, rarely causes joint injuries. Once past an initial conditioning period, you can go out for rides of two to four hours day after day, consuming enormous numbers of calories without fear of the biomechanical overstress injuries that often plague runners. All-day rides are common; experienced tourists can cover more than 100 miles a day for weeks on end. That represents a daily caloric consumption rate of about 4,000, approximately equal to the energy needed to run 40 miles. Because of this, cycling is the ideal high-volume training method. Those long rides are fun, too. They can be taken to scenic local places out of reach of the runner unless he drives there, something that is increasingly unattractive as fuel costs rise.

Thanks to the fact that cycling is not a weight-bearing activity, the lower incidence of injury means that riders can avoid the layoffs many runners suffer from time to time. The key to lifetime fitness is consistent lifetime exercise. The more time you spend injured and unable to exercise, the more time you will have to devote to the frustrating and lengthy chore of merely regaining lost conditioning. Even worse, a hurt athlete tends to rush back into training too fast following recovery, thus predisposing himself to yet another injury and layoff. Some typical runners'

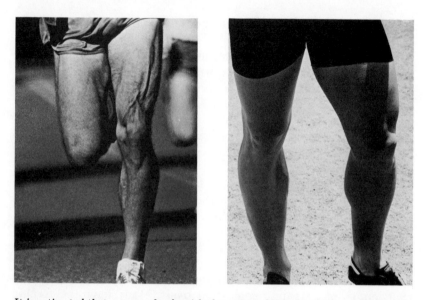

It is estimated that a runner lands with three times his body weight on each stride. It's no wonder, then, why even days of easy running may not do much to relieve soreness and help stress injuries mend. In fact, it could make things worse. Cyclists, on the other hand, have a significantly lower incidence of joint and muscle problems than runners. An obvious conclusion is that many injury-prone runners would be better off physically (and quite likely psychologically) if they rode a bike on their light/short days instead of pounding the pavement again. What's more, the smooth, non-weight-bearing action of pedaling can actually speed recovery because it increases blood circulation in the legs. And when done properly, a cycling workout will produce as much physiological benefit as equal time spent running.

problems, like chondromalacia, can become chronic, degenerative and in some cases preclude further activity. Cyclists, on the other hand, can follow a moderate but consistent routine week after week over the years with a significantly lower incidence of disabling injuries. The result is superior fitness as well as greater peace of mind.

My own case is illustrative. In 13 years of hard training and racing, the only cycling injury that has kept me off the bike for longer than one day was a crash in my first season (not the fault of the activity but rather my own inexperience). I lost some skin and cut my elbow badly, but was able to resume riding in a week. Otherwise, those 13 years have been remarkably injury-free, even though I often push to my limits on mountainous one-day rides or in races.

However, during this same period I have had two extensive layoffs due to knee injuries from running. The worst thing was that I could neither run nor ride, even though the injury was due solely to running. This doesn't include many other aches and strains that precluded running but allowed me to continue to ride. Without cycling to fall back on, I would have been forced to severely limit my exercise or stop entirely.

This is not to deprecate running as a fitness or competitive activity. I enjoy running and have trained and competed at distances from two miles to the marathon. However, I realize that when I run I risk long, frustrating and debilitating layoffs. On the bike that worry is practically nonexistent.

Don't fear the machinery

An apprehension that many non-cyclists have about the sport is that it requires great mechanical skill and big outlays of time to keep the bike properly maintained. Running is so much easier, they argue, because all you have to do is lace on your shoes and go. Maybe. But it seems to me that runners, including myself, spend considerable time maintaining their personal machinery: ice on the knee after a run and heat on assorted aches, not to mention the daily ritual of applying sole cement so the angle of heelstrike will remain precise. I am a terrible mechanic with no discernible talent for the skills of bike maintenance. However, I do almost all the work on the five bikes my wife and I own, and I've had no more training than what comes out of a repair manual. If I can do it, anyone can.

Some cyclists go overboard here and give the impression that the bike is an arcane device requiring obsessive care. One of my early memories of bike racing was the sight of a Veteran rider's post-race maintenance. He had no sooner crossed the finish line than he pulled what appeared to be a complete bike shop out of his van. He clamped the bike into a portable stand and began to disassemble the whole thing right there in the parking lot. While other riders were still flushed with the excitement of the race, comparing notes on who made the break and who got dropped, this guy was polishing his chainrings with a toothbrush and wiping flecks of dried perspiration off the top tube. It was the sort of fastidious attention to detail I had theretofore associated with operating room personnel in charge of sterility. I remember deciding that if this ritual was necessary, I didn't need the sport. Fortunately, it isn't.

Along with most riders, I steadfastly cling to the belief that a bike doesn't have to be shined and lubed to perfection to perform well. I have a bike to ride, not to polish. Yet with simple maintenance procedures and inspections done at regular intervals,

I have had no mechanical problems on the road for many years. Don't let the machine frighten you away. The bicycle is a benevolent piece of technology that simply adds a new dimension to human performance.

Prospective riders frequently rebel against the cost of cycling. Of course the sport is more expensive than running, but there are ways to lessen the outlay, as detailed in the chapter on clothing and equipment. The point here is that you don't need to make a big investment to use cycling for fitness and, contrary to popular belief, you can get race-worthy equipment for a modest sum. When it comes down to it, if you are injured and can't run, you need a bike so you can exercise consistently. The price of a decent 10-speed is small indeed when you consider how much your health is worth.

Ride to overcome running injuries

If you are presently a runner who suffers from chronic injury, you certainly don't have to give up your sport entirely; cycling may make you healthier and even faster afoot. How can it help? Consider: The No. 1 enemy of the runner is overstress. Too much hard running and the body will fail to adapt, leading first to slowed improvement and eventually to injury. On the other hand, only quality work will produce the kind of adaptation necessary for racing success. This means that serious runners tread a fine line between productive work and breakdown, and the best approach seems to be an alternation of hard training days with easy ones. Yet this system, advocated by Bowerman and Osler and others, has a built-in disadvantage: The same tendons, muscles and ligaments are being stressed every day. It is only the degree of stress, not the location, that is altered in a hard/easy program.

For example, how often have you or someone you know run a hard 20 miles in training or gone all out in a race with no hint of trouble, only to have a crippling injury appear several days later during a short recovery run? We are often on the threshold of injury. The easy runs that should help stimulate recovery through increased blood flow to fatigued muscles can often aggravate strained tendons and ligaments. The answer to this dilemma is to alternate the hard running days with an hour or so of easy spinning on the bike.

Such a combination will help a runner's mental attitude as well as his physical recovery. Athletes get addicted to their sports until it is virtually impossible to take a day off. Runners visualize themselves gaining weight and losing hard-won form at the very mention of the rest they need. Cycling can lessen the chances of injury while still satisfying the craving for aerobic work.

Variety is another important psychological plus. Overtraining is both a physiological and psychological process. The runner who feels tired and begins to dread training may have gone too far physically, or he may be mentally burned out. Instead of missing workouts and losing form until enthusiasm returns, he could vary his training with several days of long, steady rides. The bike will enable him to get away from the usual running routes as it gives the physiological benefits of continued exercise. Even better, staleness can be avoided altogether by routinely alternating running and cycling.

Much has been made in running publications about the need to strengthen the quadriceps. Arthur Lydiard, for example, advocates hill running as a means of developing more power and endurance in these thigh muscles responsible for extending the leg. Yet it is also recognized that hill running can lead to injury. Also, some parts of the country have no hills worthy of the name. Cycling, however, is a notorious developer of quadriceps power. Look at the legs of serious cyclists compared to those of runners — most riders have fuller, more defined muscles and better vascularity. They seem to exude power. If a runner trains on the bike he will have the snap needed when the hills and miles get long. As a bonus, pedaling develops the vastus medialis, the muscle on the lower inside of the thigh that is vital to proper tracking of the kneecap. This strengthening can help a runner avoid chondromalacia.

Swimming is often the exercise suggested for the incapacitated runner, but pools can be crowded and workouts may be difficult to schedule since they cannot be done by simply going out the back door. Often overlooked is the fact that many runners either don't swim well enough to get much benefit or they have so little body fat they sink like a rock. Cycling can be a much better interim conditioner. Many injuries that make running impossible do not seem to be affected by the pedaling motion. For instance, I am subject to chronic pain on the outside of the knee when I boost my running mileage too abruptly, but I can cycle without discomfort even when I can barely walk. Cycling enables me to retain my fitness as well as pump more blood to the problem area to promote healing.

A more famous example of how cycling can help the injured runner is Alberto Salazar, who got tendinitis and had to quit running for eight weeks before the 1980 Olympic Trials. Part of his alternate fitness program consisted of two sessions daily on a stationary bike, totaling 80 minutes. He was able to get his heart rate up to 175, about what he achieved with running intervals. At least partially because of this cycling, he was able to make the Olympic team at 10,000 meters with a personal best time in spite of the extensive layoff from running. This indicates that cycling not only allows a runner to maintain pre-injury form but even improve upon it.

A better sport for many runners?

Beyond the training and therapeutic benefits, there is another reason for you to consider cycling. If you are a moderately successful competitive runner who can't crack the top ranks, maybe you are in the wrong sport. Perhaps cycling is where your talent really lies.

Look at it this way: You and I and millions of other runners in the U.S. are struggling to become more competitive, training hard day after day to run times that our more gifted counterparts achieve easily. The hard fact is that very few athletes can be outstanding distance runners; there are any number of uncontrollable and insurmountable reasons why the great majority of us can't.

Most of us don't have the body type for greatness. Even at less than 10% body fat, we have too much muscle and too large a bone structure to get down to the two-pounds-per-inch-of-height figure often said necessary for successful running. If we diet to force our stubborn flesh into a physical mold we don't fit, we lose muscle as well as fat — we get weaker and slower. And because dieting demands will power and psychic energy that is better conserved for use in quality workouts, we become two-time losers. The flesh is weak and the mind isn't willing. However, in cycling the bike carries all body weight. If you are big-boned and muscular you may have trouble on extended climbs, but you may make up for it with great power on the flats as well as a feared sprint. Cycling has a niche for nearly every body type.

Another problem involves the biomechanical imbalances in our feet, legs, hips and back. Expensive orthotics and stretching exercises help, but usually they just postpone the inevitable breakdown. Without such safety measures you might get injured at 20 miles a week; with them you can go 40. But the guy up the street can run 60 miles week after week with no pain, do it faster than you, and in races you haven't finished close to him yet. On the bike, however, you can align your foot on the pedal precisely by adjusting the cleats on your cycling shoes. This, along with the fact that pedaling is not a jarring movement, practically eliminates biomechanical problems.

Additionally, most of us don't have the neuromuscular wiring that allows the effortless, gliding stride of a Bill Rodgers. We clunk along, a genetic disaster, trying vainly to do something we were never intened to do well, mocked by our own unreachable goals and frustrated beyond words in the attempt to be what we aren't. How long would a 130-pound marathoner's body type last in a football game? Yet many people with natural physical equipment unsuited for running try to run marathons, then blame some flaw of character or motivation or training when they get hurt or fail to meet predetermined and usually unrealistic goals.

Of course, not everyone can be a champion cyclist, either. But it occurs to me that many of the current middle-of-the-pack runners may be in the wrong kind of race. At least you can usually find your true potential in cycling because the gentler nature of the activity will enable you to train consistently. You can explore your cardiovascular, mental and muscular limits, not those placed upon you by a weak Achilles tendon or some quirk in the tracking of your patella in the femoral groove. If you are a runner who is increasingly frustrated, either by injury or because you can't excel, my advice is to give cycling a try. You've already got a good aerobic base from which to develop.

Learning from racing cyclists

If you intend to keep running as your No. 1 sport but I've convinced you to ride — at least a little — why should you read this book about starting out in bike racing? After all, what you are seeking is a complementary means of conditioning. The answer is that riders with fitness as their goal can learn a great deal from competitors. This is hard to believe for many recreational riders who perceive racing as a completely separate activity requiring a more aggressive mental attitude and a far superior level of fitness, but it's true.

For one thing, racers know how to handle bad weather. Cycling has been criticized because rain and snow can disrupt the training schedule. I agree that it is harder and more dangerous to ride in bad weather than it is to run, but most cyclists could ride in far worse conditions than they do and even find it enjoyable. Racers know that in order to get in the miles they have to get out on the road. So they dress warmly in old clothes and simply do it. They also know that bikes won't rust away or melt if they get wet. When they come home from a sloppy ride they merely hose off the machinery and hang it in its usual place to dry. Then they squirt some lubrication on the chain, cables and the pivot points of the brakes and derailleurs. It takes about five minutes. That, plus some periodic repacking of the internal bearings, is all that is needed.

The biggest problem that keeps the casual rider indoors is lack of commitment. The racer knows he has to get out, but the fitness fan doesn't feel the same motivation. However, even hard-core racers, accustomed to training with icicles on their down tubes, know that in some conditions even they can't get a good workout. Examples are during severe cold that could cause frostbite or when roads are covered with snow or ice. Under such circumstances, racers are found indoors riding on rollers, ergometers or wind-load simulators like the Racer-Mate or Turbo Trainer. Runners who also ride may be better off doing likewise rather than slogging it out in the snow or darkness to the detriment of their health.

Another lesson racers and racing can teach is proper riding position and pedaling technique. The competitor works long hours developing the ability to spin a low gear smoothly and easily. As Seattle cyclist Jerry Baker says, "If you can't spin a little gear, then you probably can't spin a big one." As we saw when my friend the injured runner was forced onto his bike, many casual riders commit the double sin of coupling a large gear with a slow cadence. As a result they don't get the workout they should. The big gear makes their leg muscles ache and throb, and the quick fatigue doesn't allow them to keep their heart rate at the training-effect level long enough. In addition, they run the risk of straining tendons and ligaments. Better to emulate the racers who smoothly pedal a moderate gear at 90-110 r.p.m. This sufficiently raises the heart rate without blowing away the quadriceps and knees.

Finally, mass-start racing requires solid bike-handling skills. Racers develop the ability to stay upright by training in groups, honing the reflexes needed to corner properly, ride a straight line and bump into other cyclists without tensing up. Because some bike-handling ability is necessary for the fitness rider, take a tip from the racer and work on these techniques in groups and by yourself. You'll ride with greater confidence.

The rest of this book talks about how to develop the training program and skills necessary for being a good rider. Although it is addressed to the aspiring bike racer, nearly everything is applicable to you as a runner/cyclist in search of superior fitness. But don't be surprised if, after you have ridden awhile with increasing enjoyment and strength, you get the urge to try racing. If you do, you'll be entering a sport that is on the brink of a popularity explosion in the U.S. as thousands of athletes discover the thrill of going fast under their own power.

It's not expected that a dedicated runner would want to immediately get involved in full-fledged sanctioned cycling events — the outlay of money for necessary clothing and race-worthy equipment can be significant when starting from scratch. And it is likely that even a very fit runner would need to put in many miles before being competitive, due to the fundamental differences between a bike race and a running race. The runner can go at his own pace and attempt to break his personal record for the distance or course, doing this with little regard to those around him. The drafting effect in cycling, however, makes it virtually imperative that you have the strength and riding skills to stay with the pack. Because several cyclists taking turns breaking the wind can go faster than a single rider who has to do all the work himself, once you are off the back the race may as well be over. As a result, cyclists within a particular race category are usually more evenly matched than runners.

On the other hand, there is a kind of bike racing that not only avoids the intricacies of group riding but also has physiological benefits for the runner. This is time trialing, individual rides against the clock. Each competitor leaves the start at a set interval and no drafting is allowed. Races are usually held on a flat, out-and-back course. Best of all, bike clubs are increasingly sponsoring TTs as midweek, low-key races open to anyone — no special equipment or U.S. Cycling Federation license is required. The advantages of time trials for the serious runner are extensive, including the development of leg power, the chance to meet new people involved in a different by physiologically similar sport, and the fun of exploring a new competitive opportunity. Time trials combine the safety of running events with the speed and smoothness of cycling, and they are not hard to prepare for and ride well, as I'll discuss in subsequent chapters.

PART
II

Machinery

Mechanical and Human

6
Equipment
Bike racing can be expensive,
but here are ways to cut the cost

BIKE RACING HAS a reputation as an expensive sport. It's a fact that many a prospective competitor never gets started because he is afraid of not being able to make the necessary investment.

Such fears aren't eased by those who show up at training rides astride a custom frame equipped with the latest titanium components, the price tag pushing $2,000. Tell the aspiring cyclist that good racing tires cost more than those on his car and he'll take up running in a hurry. The mistaken assumption that you have to be rich to be a bicycle racer is perpetuated by the belief that quality of equipment correlates directly with performance. You might believe it after reading the sales pitches in cycling publications, but such emphasis reflects the hard economic facts of advertising more than it does the necessity of all those exotic components for the beginner.

The cyclist himself is not blameless, though. Improvement is difficult and requires work, discipline and a certain amount of heavy breathing. It is more pleasant to think about how much faster you would instantly become if only you had that frame or this pair of pedals. For the novice it hardly matters. It's the motor, not the bike, and as a beginner you are far better off spending your time on training rather than shopping. Not to mention the expense — that money is going to be needed for travel to races.

Jim Moody is a good case to consider. While in his 30s, he began racing as a Senior IV on a standard clincher-tired touring bike. At the end of the season he was the Colorado Road Champion, though on a better cycle. But talent, enthusiasm and a carefully structured training program were more important in his initial races than mechanical details. Almost any 10-speed in good working order can be made adequate for getting started. There will be plenty of time later for better bikes and components.

You don't need a $1,500 bike like U.S. professional Tom Broznowski in order to compete. Even a modest budget can equip you with the essentials: strong, light racing wheels; cleats and toe clips (or a binding system); a good saddle; quality sidepull brakes; and a helmet and shorts.

So in spite of all you may have heard, it is possible to enter racing and be competitive on a fairly modest investment. The trick is knowing where you can get away with cheaper equipment and where settling for less is false economy. If you are presently a recreational rider or perhaps a runner who is thinking about giving competitive cycling a try, you can do it without selling the farm. Here are some suggestions for cutting the cost of many items you'll need, and how to economize when it comes time to replace present equipment. The prices I've listed are averages based on various 1986 retail catalogs.

RIDING ATTIRE

Shoes

Shoes are very important in cycling because they are the link between your leg power and the bike. They help you avoid knee injuries because the cleats can be positioned to align feet on the pedals, ensuring that the knee joint moves correctly in biomechanical terms. The cleats also allow power to be exerted on the upstroke, making round, efficient pedaling possible. Some beginners use running shoes or cleatless models designed for riders who get off the bike frequently to walk around, but for serious training and racing you must have the comfort and efficiency that only cleated cycling shoes provide.

To save money on this vital investment it is possible to buy used shoes through a shop or club. But be sure they are in relatively good repair and that you adjust the cleats or install new ones to fit your own physiological idiosyncrasies. If you are buying new shoes, choose the lowest priced model that offers a stiff sole — important for transmitting power and preventing foot fatigue and numbness. Even budget shoes ($35; some models cost twice as much) should get you through a full season. You can later purchase better ones if you decide that cycling is for you, using the first pair for riding in sloppy weather. It's a good idea to get shoes pre-drilled for the Look pedal system even if you are now using conventional pedals. If you make the conversion, it will be easier to mount the cleats.

Shorts

You will need at least two pairs of chamois-lined shorts so you can always have one clean and ready for the next ride. Cycling shorts should always be black, for two reasons: (1) they give you the perfect place to wipe off greasy hands; (2) potentially embarrassing stains from the saddle won't show. The chamois inside the crotch should be big, soft and have no seams that could cause irritation. It is painful and frustrating to ride on saddle sores, a malady that poorly designed shorts or a dirty chamois practically guarantee.

You will save money over several years if you buy shorts made of the toughest material you can find. Sturdy Lycra material seems to work just fine but other riders are big boosters of wool/nylon blends or polypropylene. At about $30 either choice is a least $5 cheaper than traditional all-wool shorts, which tend to wear out sooner. Actually, the first thing to go is usually the chamois. If you buy replacements ($10) and sew in a new one when needed, you can extend the life of the shorts far beyond what is normal.

Suspenders ($5) are a good idea because shorts with an elastic waistband have a way of drooping while those held up by a drawstring can feel like a tourniquet. Buy suspenders which are about an inch wide and have a nylon face in the clasps to keep rust and damage to the fabric at a minimum. Some colored suspenders will bleed dye into your jersey and skin when you perspire, so white is the safest choice.

Helmets

Hardshell helmets should be worn during training and they are required for USCF-sanctioned racing. You can save money by buying a traditional leather strap model, but it won't save your life. On the other hand, a hardshell model costs twice as much (up to $75) but it can make the difference in being able to get up and walk away after a severe blow to a head. Be wary of used hardshells, though, because they may have been crashed; some are lined with crushable foam which is good for only one impact before the helmet has to be reconditioned or replaced. Of the various plastic helmets on the market, those made by Bailen, Bell, MSR, Pro-tec and Skid-Lid have scored well in product tests. My personal recommendation for racers is the Bell V1-Pro, based on lightness and ventilation. Whichever helmet you choose, it is essential that it fits correctly and comfortably and that you wear it every time you ride.

Jerseys

Your clothing needs can be purchased economically or picked out of your current wardrobe. Look for a polyester jersey ($25).

Perhaps no wheel would survive the impact that destroyed this one, but expensive damage is more likely when lightness is put ahead of strength and durability in the selection of rims, spokes, and tires. And speaking of damage, you can see why good quality hardshell helmets are now required in amateur racing instead of the leather-strap style shown here.

All-wool and wool blends do a better job of wicking perspiration away from the skin, making them both cooler in the summer and warmer in winter, but they also cost more ($35). It's an unnecessary expense if you have a wool T-shirt ($15) to wear underneath. Keep an eye out for used jerseys at thrift stores or bike shops. If you join a club, a nice jersey might come with the dues or at wholesale price. Make sure the cut is long enough in back so that it doesn't ride up and expose bare skin when you are down on the drops.

Since cycling jerseys are a benefit primarily because of the rear pockets, you can save money by sewing some on a pullover. It'll work fine for training and even racing until you choose to invest in a good jersey. Three pockets are best because when you are carrying something heavy, such as a full water bottle, you can put it in the middle to keep it from tugging around to the side.

Gloves

Padded cycling gloves ($12) will help prevent hands from going numb on long rides, and they protect against abrasions if you crash. Even the most minor, slow-speed accident can injure the palms since it is instinctive to break a fall with outstretched hands. Look for gloves with a mesh back for good ventilation and moisture absorption. Velcro closures are another nice feature. Any cycling glove will wear out quickly if you use the palm to wipe debris off your tires as you ride along, so a useful substitute at half the price is a pair of leather work gloves with the fingers cut off. If you punch some holes in the back they will be as cool as their fancy counterparts. If you are patient and skilled you could even sew some foam padding on the palms and cover it with the leather from the gloves' amputated fingers. However, if you have padded handlebar sleeves extra cushioning in the gloves isn't needed.

Winter clothing

Cycling attire for cold weather is expensive and often hard to get, but clothing that works almost as well is as near as your closet or local sporting goods store. Instead of the long wool tights that sell for $40 or more, use $10 cotton/polyester sweat pants, the kind with the drawstring waist and elastic cuffs. Choose dark blue or black rather than a lighter color so stains won't show. Be sure the legs are long enough to stay down around your ankles throughout the pedal stroke. Since sweat pants are usually cut full, you may have to pin over the excess material on the lower right leg so it doesn't foul on your chainrings. Wear your chamois shorts underneath and, if it's really cold, add long underwear.

On top, wear a light nylon windbreaker with a zipper front over assorted old sweat shirts and pullovers, which insulate better than a single heavy garment. Make one a turtleneck for throat protection. I use an old running suit top with pockets sewed on the back so I can carry food on longer rides and stow the windbreaker if it warms up. If you wear a wool or polypro T-shirt next to your skin you will be warmer, especially after you begin to perspire — by wicking away moisture it helps prevent freeze-out on descents or headwind sections. The old trick of layering several sheets of newspaper between shirts provides extra insulation and stops the wind. Crumple the sheets first so they will be flexible and stay in place. Be careful that you don't wear a good shirt under the paper because the ink will smudge after becoming damp.

Protecting the head, hands and feet is the key to keeping warm. Tape or plug the vent holes in your helmet and use an ear band or stocking cap under it. Wear the same lined leather gloves that you have for outside work. At moderate temperatures you can use duct tape to cover the vent holes in your shoes; when it gets colder pull old wool socks over everything, cutting out small windows to expose the cleats. Bind the edge of the holes with strapping tape and then sew it firmly in place so the socks don't stretch or tear. I use old mountaineering rag socks with heels too worn to wear in my climbing boots. When it's really cold put a plastic bag over each sock/shoe combination to break the wind.

Wet-weather gear

Wet weather is a bigger challenge than cold when it comes to cutting costs. Rainsuits made of the miracle fabric Gore-Tex would be ideal, but at about $150 they are outrageously expensive. The cheapest way to beat the rain is with plastic bags of assorted sizes. Put smaller ones over your shoes, and under your wind-breaker wear a larger garbage can liner with head and arm holes cut out. Most wet-weather training rides are relatively short and hard, so if you get soaked from without or within (sweat and condensation) it doesn't matter much. Save your LSD ride for a drier day.

Wearing a cloth cycling cap under the helmet is advisable so you can turn down the brim to keep rain and sleet out of your eyes. My early season rides in Colorado are always subject to sudden snow squalls. Without a bill it is sometimes nearly impossible to see where I'm going. I once had to ride home into a blizzard with one hand cocked by my forehead to shield my eyes so I could see the rapidly disappearing road. After 20 miles of that I haven't forgotten the hat since.

BICYCLE COMPONENTS

As in clothing, when it comes to equipment there are several areas where you shouldn't compromise quality. But this doesn't mean you have to buy the most expensive item on the market.

Saddles

Probably the most important component is the saddle. This nomination may surprise some riders, but my thinking is this: If your posterior feels like it is on the rack, you just aren't going to get in the miles. Flesh has its limits and the flesh that contacts the saddle is more tender than most. I have tried various models over the years but I invariably come back to a well-broken-in Brooks Professional ($35), an all-leather saddle, or a plastic based Turbo ($30). Other riders report almost immediate comfort from the new breed of anatomically designed saddles, such as those marketed by Avocet. Included are shorter, wider models made especially for women.

Like running shoes, saddle choice is a matter of how your unique physical structure fits a given design. The seat that is most comfortable for you may not be the current rage, the lightest available or even very expensive. Be sure it is wide enough to cradle your pelvic bones or you will feel like you are astride a razor blade. Correct width is the single most important factor in saddle comfort, with softness a distant second. Realize, though, that probably no seat is going to be totally comfortable in the early stages of your training if you are a new rider. It takes what is called "saddle time" to become accustomed to the unfamiliar pressures. You can help the process by making sure the saddle is correctly positioned (see chapter 2), by wearing chamois shorts and by keeping rides to a reasonable length during the first few weeks.

Instead of spending the time and money to try various designs, you can make some modifications to the saddle you have if it seems less than satisfactory. First look under the nose to see if there is a tension bolt that can be used to vary the softness. If there is none and you have a leather-covered plastic model that is too hard, you can carefully drill a series of holes in the shell. Remove the saddle and drill up from the bottom, being careful not to go into the layer of padding or leather. Pattern the holes so that the shell is made more flexible in the areas of greatest contact. On a rock-hard, all-plastic seat you can drill right through and/or use contact cement to attach a closed-cell foam like Ensolite. Using a razor blade, bevel and shape the material after you glue it down. The Spenco material developed for running shoe insoles makes an effective extra pad that is less bulky.

Freewheels and chains

Another component that is short on glamor but essential for performance is a freewheel appropriate for your needs. Quite a few bikes that are otherwise suitable for racing come equipped with wide-ratio freewheels, 14-28 or worse, that will handicap you in any competition except the Mt. Washington Hill Climb. A seven speed like the Ultra Seven or Regina CX-S in 13-14-15-16-17-19-21, coupled with the standard chainwheel setup of 52-42, will be right for the terrain in most road races. For time trials and flat criteriums you should have a 12-18 or 13-19 straight block. Go for a basic five-speed freewheel ($15) — or smoother, six-speed model ($30) — and forget alloy models. They sell for about $100 and are not as durable as steel. The ounces saved are meaningless for most riders. While the freewheel change is being made don't fail to discard the spoke protector if the bike is so equipped.

Few things in life are certain, but to death and taxes you can add the need to replace a worn chain whenever installing a new freewheel, and vice versa. This is because these two power train components wear together and there will be roughness or skipping if a new partner enters the relationship. It's no financial catastrophe, though, because for about $7 you can buy the chain many riders rate at the top in shifting smoothness and wearability, the Sedisport.

Derailleurs

In most cases the derailleurs on your bike, especially the front changer, will be adequate for training and racing. The major exception is when the rear derailleur is a touring model made to handle the wide-ratio freewheels just mentioned. It will still work with the closer ratios you change to, but the long-cage design isn't needed and will only result in slower and less precise shifting. Keep that derailleur and original freewheel for your vacation to the mountains, or see if your local dealer will give you a trade-in allowance on the new equipment.

The choices are many when it comes to rear derailleurs and you needn't spend upwards of $50 to get one with the quick, positive action needed for racing. The SunTour VX is a good performer for about $15 and so are similarly priced models made by Simplex and Shimano, among others. Although low-cost derailleurs tend to become sloppy as the months go by, they will be fine for at least the first season. Also, you won't be out much money if the worst happens and you tear one up in a crash.

Gear shift levers belong on the down tube. If your bike's are mounted on the stem you will find it next to impossible to make snappy gear changes when in a low riding position. Either invest the $20 it costs for new down tube levers or see if the local shop has a used set; maybe you can make an even-up trade. Don't let yourself be talked into buying handlebar-end shifters ($20). All that extra cable and housing results in an indistinct feel for what is going on at the derailleur end, and it is easy for someone to give you an unwanted gear change in the middle of a crowded racing pack. A few good riders use handlebar-end shifters but beginners will be much better off with levers on the down tube; the hand naturally drops to that position when taken off the bars, and the chances of making a quick, precise shift are better.

Wheels and tires

I agree with the recommendation of equipment theorists in one respect: You do need good wheels and tires for racing. But durability comes first, not light weight, even though it is true that the weight of rotating components is far more important than that of stationary ones, such as the saddle. If you succumb to the superlight fetish and use sub-300-gram rims with 28 spokes and featherweight tires you are asking for trouble. Not only will such wheels be less likely to withstand the rigors of hard accelerations and bad roads, they may flex in corners and give a mushy ride.

Good wheels are expensive but there are some alternatives. You might be able to safely buy a used pair if you can get them from a shop or person you trust. Go over them carefully to check for trueness, roundness, dings, cracks, rounded-off nipples, etc. and take a look inside the hubs. Building your own wheels is possible and it'll save a hefty labor charge, but it requires considerable knowledge and special equipment. I prefer to lace up new wheels, then have them tensioned and trued by the professional mechanic at the shop. The charge is less than for building a whole wheel.

Tires are the racer's biggest ongoing equipment expense. Although high-pressure clinchers are nearly as good as tubulars in many ways, I neverthless recommend tubulars (sew-ups) for racing. It is not only a question of speed but of riding pleasure. Tubulars seem more lively and responsive. Also, clincher rims still outweigh equally durable tubular rims by 50 to 75 grams each. However, good racing tubulars are now up to $30 or $40 each and the price seems to be climbing faster than Greg LeMond in the Alps, so a great many top racers are now competing as well as training on clinchers, a trend I expect will continue.

One advantage of racing on clinchers is their low rolling resistance which, according to some studies, makes up for the greater rim weight in all types of riding except a short sprint. You can save some money with clinchers because perfectly adequate tires are around $15 compared to twice that for tubulars. On the other hand, you can pay up to $35 each for state-of-the-art clinchers. So if you want the best you still have to pay the piper.

Clinchers are much easier to mount and repair than tubulars: no more messing around with stickly glue jobs. And, for training, clinchers have the advantage of allowing you nearly unlimited punctures en route. With tubulars if you puncture twice you end up walking because no one carries two spares. On clinchers, though, you can tote a spare tube and a patch kit. Unless you completely rupture the tire casing, you can always throw on another patch and keep riding.

I now train almost exclusively on clinchers and race on tubulars but as of this writing I am down to only one pair of sew-up wheels.

As the other ones have been damaged, I've rebuilt them as clinchers. So it may not be long before I'm a convert.

Don't try to save money on rim cement ($1.50/tube) by skimping on how much you use, buying a bargain brand or using what is known as double-sided tacky tape. Rolling a tire is painful and costly, and if it happens during a USCF race and causes other riders to crash it is grounds for suspension.

Brakes

Expensive brakes perform better than inexpensive ones, but the difference is often overrated. Even budget brakes can work fine if they are kept in adjustment and you stiffen them up by installing thicker cables and better pads, such as Mathauser ($8/set). However, top-line sidepulls such as Campagnolo's ($150) and the somewhat less expensive imitations are superior in several ways, ease of adjustment being a primary one. Most low-cost sidepull models are devilishly hard to keep centered. Inexpensive centerpulls don't have that problem, but their systems may flex so much that braking precision is lost.

In the last several years I have used — in descending level of price — Campagnolo, Universal 68 sidepulls, Universal 61 centerpulls and Weinmann 500 sidepulls. All were adequate and the cheapest of the lot, the Weinmanns ($25), are also very light. But nothing quite equals the quick and positive feel of top-line brakes, and this certainly increases confidence.

Should your bike be equipped with so-called safety brake levers, get rid of them. They may be okay for sidewalk cruising but are useless for a serious rider. If you are lucky it will be possible to remove the extension arms and keep the main levers, over which you can install gum rubber hoods ($5/pair) for hand comfort. If you're not lucky, check around to see if anyone wants to swap their regular levers for your safety set before you buy new ones (about $15).

Pedals

Any pair of pedals is fine as long as toe clips and straps can be attached and they can accept your shoe cleats. If new pedals are needed, Japanese copies of the Campagnolo Record road model ($60) abound for less than $25 a pair. You can go under $15 for decent pedals if you accept a little extra weight for a steel rather than alloy cage.

The newly developed strapless systems like the Look or the Adidas are quite a bit more expensive (around $100). But they do seem to be an improvement over traditional pedals and seem to be gaining rapidly in popularity.

Steel toe clips sell for about $5 a pair and are more durable than their $9 alloy counterparts. Buy the length that allows the ball of your foot to be directly above the pedal axle. Toe straps are an item worth spending extra money on because the thin leather and weak buckles on inexpensive models ($3) often can't handle the forces you will be applying. You must be able to count on straps to not stretch and let your feet pull out during hard, off-the-saddle efforts. Also, cheap buckles have a way of making the straps feel too tight or too loose, rarely just right. If you will be using the same pedals for all your riding, you might want to splurge for Binda Extras ($8) or another brand built the same way. The strap is an easily identifiable leather/nylon/leather sandwich.

Cranksets

The crank arms, chainwheels and bottom bracket assembly combine to make a high-cost component. Campagnolo's best crankset goes for about $200, but Sugino makes a close copy that will be fine for your racing and sells for a third as much. Although you can buy alloy cotterless cranksets for less than $70, it probably isn't possible to do it and still have something that won't flex and creak excessively when you are applying the power. There is also the matter of the chainwheels starting out true and remaining that way, an important factor in how well the front derailleur will function.

However, there is usually no need to replace even a steel cottered crankset to have a suitable bike for beginning racing. As long as the bottom bracket movement is lubricated properly and in adjustment it will spin efficiently and serve you well. Remove and discard the chainguard if there is one and see that the large chainwheel has 52 teeth and the small 42 or 40. If yours doesn't, you should replace them with these sizes, which are what most of your road racing competitors will be using. If your crankset is in good shape except for wobbling chainwheels, a shop mechanic should be able to put them into good true.

Frames

The frame is the most expensive single component of a racing bike. In recent years cyclists have been demanding more and more stiffness on the theory that more energy will be converted into forward motion and less will be absorbed by the frame. This has resulted in shorter wheelbases, steeper angles and the idea that anything less than a 74-degree head and seat tube isn't suitable for racing. Nonsense.

If you are a beginning competitor, use what you have and don't buy an expensive frame for your first couple of seasons. You will probably have more crashes in races and training during this learning period than you will later, so why have them on a $500 frame? And consider this: Coppi and other great pro riders of the 1940s and '50s raced throughout their careers on frames that were longer and shallower than anything now in vogue, and they were even equipped with steel components and cottered cranks. This sort of frame, derided by the purist today as suitable only for touring, is still adequate in most racing events. It may even be superior in long races on rough pavement where a little more comfort and stability can help the rider relax.

Look for a secondhand frame from racers who are moving on to a different model. Be sure that the frame fits you and check to see that it tracks properly. Don't trust a seller who swears on a stack of tubulars that the frame has never been crashed. Take it to a reliable builder or shop and have it checked. An out-of-line frame will cause insuperable handling problems. The shop can also inspect the lug work and tubes for cracks and signs of impending failure.

Don't be afraid of a used touring frame. If it has been made in the last 10 years or so it is probably reasonably tight and it'll be fine for your initial racing. If you want a better frame later, the first one can always be used as a second bike for training in bad weather or for cyclocross.

It is entirely possible that your present bike, which you may have been tempted to discount as too cheap and heavy for racing, will be quite adequate after the alterations I've been suggesting. A rider I know had cruised around on a Raleigh Super Course that he bought in 1973 for about $150. It had Reynolds straight gauge main tubes and a 41-inch wheelbase. When he began racing he upgraded the brake pads, changed the inner chainring from 38 to 42 and went to tubular wheels. He then competed on this bike for two years with plenty of success.

Finally, watch garage sales for old frames and bikes that are suitable for racing. Often these can be bought cheaper than from a racer because the seller may not realize what he has. Occasionally a vintage Bianchi or some other classic will crop up at secondhand stores, yard sales or flea markets in ethnic neighborhoods of cities. Such old frames are not merely of historical interest — if they were good enough for Coppi, they are good enough for you. As an example, Jim Meyers won a Veterans National Championship on a 21-year-old frame.

ACCESSORIES

There are some miscellaneous items that aren't strictly necessary for racing but are useful. A car rack ($50 to $200) to carry your bike is one. You can often fabricate a substitute using an existing luggage rack. Always transport the bike on the roof or trunk top, never on the bumper where even a slight traffic mishap will crush it. To be even safer, carry the bike inside the car. Pull the wheels, tie up the chain to the brake bridge with an old toe strap and put everything into plastic garbage sacks to keep grease off the upholstery.

A good wristwatch is necessary for intervals, time trials, counting cadence and knowing the elapsed time of a ride. It need not be expensive; several of the plastic digital chronographs with a stopwatch function cost less than $30. They are accurate and quite durable, though it might be wise to pay a little extra for one that is guaranteed water resistant.

It also pays to buy a bicycle computer. The Avocet model is around $30 but tells you speed, mileage, and elapsed time without cluttering up your bike. More sophisticated models report your pedal cadence, your average speed, or even your heart rate. But the additional information comes at a premium price: $50 to $100 or more.

It is important to have the tools needed for routine bike maintenance. You can, of course, take the work to the local shop, but doing it yourself has at least four advantages: (1) Even though you have to buy the necessary tools and lubricants, doing your own work will save you money as the months go by; (2) You can adjust components exactly the way you want them and have nobody to blame but yourself if something goes wrong; (3) You can do the work immediately when it's needed instead of losing valuable riding time during the several days the bike is in the shop; (4) You come to know your bike better and understand just how the mechanical aspect relates to riding performance.

Many of the tools you will need are already in the house or can be purchased at reasonable prices in a hardware store. The general tools include screwdrivers, adjustable wrenches, metric allen and open-end wrenches, and pliers with a cable cutter. You will also need some specialized tools to fit your particular components: a crank puller, headset and bottom bracket tools, a freewheel puller, cone wrenches and a chain breaker. Don't skimp on these because you'll just have to buy more after you bend up flimsy ones. Also, cheap, ill-fitting tools can result in damaged alloy components. Good tools aren't that expensive and their cost can be spread out over a year if you buy them as needed for specific maintenance jobs. A good bike shop should carry all the special tools you'll need.

I suggest that you invest in a good frame-mount pump like Silca or Zefal, either new ($12) or used. You'll thank yourself for paying a little more for quality and reliability when it keeps you from being stranded miles from home. A floor pump with built-in guage ($35) is great to have, but if your budget is tight you can put off its purchase and use the frame pump and a little muscle power. Realize, though, that a frame pump really isn't designed for daily use and will last much longer if employed only for flat tire emergencies. To keep the need for a pump to a minimum you can use tires with butyl tubes (vs. latex), which hold pressure for days.

A set of weights is needed for off-season training. Look for used ones at garage sales or secondhand stores. You only need a light set of about 100 pounds for circuit training; if you want more weight for power training, keep your eye peeled for another used set or get a local machine shop to drill scrap metal pieces with the correct size hole for your bar. Don't waste money on benches and racks. It is easy to fashion a squat rack and bench press out of 2x4s and make them sturdy enough to support the relatively light weights you will be using in high-rep training.

For winter training you'll also want a wind-load simulator for those days when you can't get out on the road or when you want a warm-up or warm-down for your weight training. Perfectly adequate models are available for around $100 and used ones show up all the time if you ask around. I like an ergometer with dropped bars and a racing saddle and pedals because you aren't sweating all over your bike when you use one. They also have variable resistance from nearly nothing to what feels like climbing Mt. Evans dragging a cement block. But good ones run around $500 so most riders either use the wind trainer or hit the ergometer at the local health club.

You get what you pay for

All these cost-cutting measures are fine for your first year or two in racing. But bear in mind that as you gain experience and move up into higher levels of competition, you will probably want to upgrade your equipment and clothing. In cycling, as in other endeavors, you get what you pay for. The long, flexible frame and cheaper tires that won't handicap you appreciably in Senior IV racing may mean the difference between success and failure in I-II events where the range of the riders' abilities is narrower. At the very least, better clothing and equipment mean more comfort and riding pleasure.

However, if you are a person of modest means it is possible to start racing without mortgaging your future. You need the patience to wait until good deals come up. You need the maturity to accept looking less like a European pro racer and more like a thrift store reject. And you need to realize that it is your training program that determines how successful you will be, not the price tag on your equipment.

7
Nutrition
*Eat a variety of foods you like
and emphasize exercise, not diet*

I APPROACH THE subject of nutrition for the racer with fear and trembling. I know of no other area so likely to produce a storm of conflict among normally sane athletes. Cyclists can be rational about equipment, training and tactics, but that calm reason deserts them in a flash when diet is mentioned. The rider who will carefully weigh the odds on his chances in a break with remarkable mental acuity becomes an opinionated bigot when asked what he eats.

Such virulent reactions stem from the nearly psychotic emphasis on food in recent years and on how it affects performance. Because of all the propaganda, many racers are convinced that diet is the secret ingredient for success and they are searching for the magic nutritional elixir that will be the key to victory. Bee pollen, vitamins, seaweed, vegetables, raw meat and other exotic substances have all been touted as the answer at one time or another.

Although the variety of diets prescribed by the experts is wide, the actual dietary practices of competitive athletes defy characterization. 1984 Olympic champion Alexi Grewal reportedly hauled suitcases of grains and nuts to Europe for his 1986 racing campaign. 1986 Tour de France winner Greg LeMond is a big fan of apple turnovers, Mexican food, and Coca-Cola. The international riders dining at the Coors Classic choose from rice, potatoes, assorted meats, vegetables, bread, and cereals. But unusual combinations are the rule. I saw a Colombian rider fuel himself for a day of racing with a huge bowl of cornflakes and bananas covered with white sugar and chocolate milk.

And then there is history's greatest speedskater, Eric Heiden, who after the Lake Placid Olympics became an instant star in cycling. He allows that he does prefer fish and fowl over red meat but he isn't overly concerned with what he eats. The biggest problem during his trips to Europe, he says, is that there's no place to buy Fritos.

Such dietary diversity need not be confusing to the beginning racer who is attempting to find his own ideal nutritional pattern. As in training techniques there are some general principles. The following dietary tips are based on a consensus of successful racers as well as nutritional experts. They represent, therefore, a blend of theory and practice. They are only guidelines; in diet, the latitude for personal preference is wider than perhaps any other area of endurance training.

Don't be a fanatic. The dietary regimen which requires iron will power is doomed to failure. Hard training and racing adds a considerable amount of stress to our lives. If rigid adherence to a diet creates more, it will not be successful for very long. Also, a fanatical approach to one diet can offend friends, alienate family and, worst of all, it may convince the racer that he will ride badly if for some reason he cannot eat his normal meal. This self-fulfilling prophecy is almost certain to occur on weekend trips to races and it has been given as one reason why U.S. international teams, faced with foreign cuisine and different standards of cleanliness, often do not do well. If adaptability is important for world-class cyclists, it is just as crucial for the domestic rider who must leave after work on Friday for a distant race, grab what he can to eat along the way, and be fueled as well as confident for an early Saturday start.

Eat in moderation. A wide variety of food, eaten in temperate amounts, will virtually ensure a balanced diet that contains proper nutrients and enables the racer to avoid the nutritional martyr syndrome that will eventually collapse. An occasional bowl of ice cream won't destroy your fitness.

It is important never to overload the stomach because such gluttony is hard on the digestive system. Like a tightly packed washing machine, the full stomach is not able to churn its contents around. The result is that the portion of the digestive process handled by the stomach is incomplete. This can lessen nutrient absorption later in the digestive process. You end up eating more but getting less benefit from it.

Chronic overeating is also involved with will power and determination. The athlete who lacks the self-discipline to decide not to overeat is unlikely to have the determination to push hard in training and racing. Every part of a rider's life influences every other part; we are a complex web of physical and mental relationships.

Big meals are a particular problem for the racer with limited time to train. Often he can ride only when able to fit the necessary time around other responsibilities, and this can mean working out quite soon after eating. If the stomach is too full a rider will be unable to do the kind of quality training that leads to improvement.

De-emphasize sugar, fat, salt and cholesterol. Excessive intake of any of these substances is generally agreed to be unnecessary and perhaps harmful, and an enormous number of calories can be eliminated from a meal if sugar and fatty spreads are avoided. For instance, a plain lettuce salad has about 20 calories. The same salad with a generous dollop of blue cheese dressing has around 120 calories and most of the addition is fat. Likewise, a piece of whole grain bread contains about 75 calories but a little added margarine and honey can easily double the figure.

Cholesterol is a problem in that nutritionists are not sure of the exact nature of the risk and to what extent exercise reduces it. Also, eggs are a vital component of the lacto-ovo-vegetarian diet, though their optimum amino acid balance is countered by their high cholesterol level. Moderation, not avoidance, seems to be the best choice here.

Emphasize carbohydrates. The endurance athlete needs to fuel his body with complex carbohydrates. This is not a difficult dietary adjustment to make because the active body craves carbohydrates and rejects excess protein and fat when training loads increase. The danger is that these carbohydrates will be ingested in the form of sugar-laden baked goods with relatively low nutritional value. Superior sources are fruits, breads, potatoes and pasta.

Healthful meals

How can these guidelines be translated into menus? Here are some good choices for the various meals.

BREAKFAST: Start with fresh fruit juice. Have some whole grain bread, toasted if you like and eaten either plain or spread with applesauce that contains no added sugar. Use honey, margarine or jam very sparingly. Cook up a whole grain cereal like rolled oats, wheat flakes, Roman Meal or a combination of grains and use non-fat or skim milk. Add a cut-up banana, peach or other fruit. If you prefer cold cereal, use a non-sweetened type like shredded wheat or Grapenuts with the same type milk and fruit. Be careful of some of the so-called natural cereals because most granolas contain excessive amounts of honey or sugar. A good alternative is a homemade mixture that combines crushed shredded wheat with Grapenuts, rolled oats, wheat germ, shredded coconut, wheat flakes and raisins. This breakfast plan avoids excess sugar and honey. It is high in carbohydrates but low in fat because it eliminates margarine or butter and features skim milk.

LUNCH: The possibilities are endless — salad of all kinds, fruit, sandwiches made of whole grain bread, lettuce, tomatoes, sprouts, sliced zucchini, low-fat cheese, etc. Have some of that rice casserole with vegetables left over from dinner. Lunch should be fairly light; most people are busy during the day and have little time for a big meal anyway. But be sure to eat enough to fuel the afternoon workout. A snack an hour or so before training might be necessary and fresh fruit is a good choice.

DINNER: The evening meal can be a problem if the rest of the family doesn't share your dietary beliefs. Compromises may be necessary but need not be extreme. Go heavy on green salad, vegetables and bread while either avoiding or eating small portions of meat, gravy, margarine, salad dressing and dessert. Liquids can be herb tea or fruit juice. For dessert or a later snack have fruit, carrots, celery and other raw vegetables. And, because man does not live by perfect nutrition alone, go ahead and get out the ice cream and cookies occasionally.

Vitamin supplements? Sure, help yourself if it makes you feel more confident that you are covering all nutritional bases. A good multiple vitamin/mineral formula derived from natural sources will cost you about a dime for each day's tablet, and that's cheap insurance. Research has shown that the water-soluble vitamins (B-complex and C) are important for the endurance athlete and most multi-vitamin formulas supply them in quantities well above the recommended minimum dosage. According to Dr. Ed Burke, writing in the comprehensive book on cycling physiology, *Inside the Cyclist,* "If an athlete does not have enough B and C vitamins, a decline in performance will be seen in a few weeks. They are needed for the production of energy and they are not stored in the body to any significant degree. When the intake is greater than the body needs, the excess is thrown out in the urine." So there is no risk in taking such supplements, and during periods of hard training and racing, especially in hot weather, they may do some good. Of course, there are excellent food sources for these vitamins

This is one rider's meal during a training camp. Cyclists have the justly deserved reputation of being among the biggest eaters in sport, but it's not gluttony. Rations like these are needed simply to keep up with the energy demands of training and racing.

as well. The Bs are found in brewer's yeast, liver and whole grain cereal; vitamin C sources include vegetables and citrus fruit and their juices.

Lest this advice rely too heavily on my own experiences, research and prejudices, I conducted an informal survey among the 10 best cyclists with whom I am personally acquainted. Not surprisingly, I found a wide range of dietary behaviors.

•Three of the 10 are highly concerned about their diets and go out of their way to eat as healthfully as possible, even to the extent of occasionally causing hard feelings when they eat at friends' houses or inconvenience when they dine out. In all cases they have the agreement and support of their families.

•Four members of the sample have modified their diets considerably over the years and have eschewed the white bread/red meat/ sugar diet in favor of more healthful forms. Although they are not afraid to alter this pattern when the situation demands it, they do so with varying degrees of guilt and misgiving.

•Two members of my sample said they eat anything and don't think about their diets at all. One proclaims loudly to anyone who will listen that his cycling is not allowed to interfere in a "normal" lifestyle, especially where eating is concerned. Both try to give the impression that they are above such concerns, that theirs is a superior talent unsullied by something as mundane as food intake. Interestingly, though, both have always eaten with variety and moderation, making their actual diets closer to those of the preceding group than they like to think or care to admit.

•One person really does eat anything and gives it no conscious thought that I can discover. He listens to my questioning or cajoling with various degrees of patience and then proceeds to eat whatever is in sight with obvious gustatory delight.

Although 10 random racers hardly constitute a statistically valid sample, I think the range is about right for the majority of cyclists. The most important observation arising from all this is that these riders will pound your ear for hours about their training plans and spend much time analyzing and evaluating their workouts regardless of their approach to diet. I suspect that the degree of improvement attainable from a maximally effective training program is much greater than that derived from an optimum diet, so long as basic nutritional needs are met.

Obviously, an atrocious diet that is deficient in vital nutrients or calories for energy is going to hamper your progress. But the difference between a sound, well-balanced diet and the theoretically perfect one is probably infinitesimal, especially when there is no agreement on what characterizes ideal nutrition.

The amount of contradictory advice in the area of the "perfect diet" is overwhelming. At some time nearly every food has been indicted as harmful — it is like the lament born of proliferating carcinogen research: everything causes cancer. For example, eggs have high cholesterol to counter their favorable amino acid compostion. Peanut butter is high in protein but also high in fat. Fiber foods like whole grains and vegetables aid elimination but may cause gas, bloating and unscheduled pit stops during training or racing. A diet devoid of meat may be ethically satisfying but can make it difficult to get the calories necessary to fuel long rides. The whole question of what elements make up a healthy diet is so complex and ultimately so ambiguous that the rider seriously interested in improving his nutrition may throw up his hands in despair. Or, given the emotion which invariably permeates such decisions, he may merely throw up.

The new racer would be wise to eat moderately, enjoyably and with variety. Concentrate on the effectiveness of your training rather than on the efficacy of your diet.

8
Slimming Down
The search for ideal body weight
is best begun during the off-season

BIKE RACERS OFTEN WORRY about how their weight affects performance — and for good reason. It is difficult to be competitive, especially in hilly events, if you are carrying extra weight. By extra I am referring to fat and also to muscle that does not directly aid the pedaling process. Every pound of body weight, regardless of its composition, contains miles of blood vessels and capillaries. And every pound needs a blood supply, which means that a set of bulging deltoids will slow you down as surely as a roll of fat around your middle.

Though some people are naturally muscular and can't get skinny no matter what they do, too much muscle is rarely a problem for beginning riders (lifetime iron pumpers excepted). However, it's your heredity, not the number of sets and reps, that determines how a weight program will affect you. Even "easy gainers" miss the point if they avoid the weight training that will help them improve.

Pitfalls of weight loss
Before attempting to pare down your excess poundage you need to be aware of two pitfalls. The first is psychological. The body produced by a power lifting program is more accepted in our society than the lean endurance look, the current craze for marathon running notwithstanding. Because most Americans are over-fat, the eye is used to rounded contours; a fit, fat-free rider looks angular and spare by comparison. It is the novice rider who usually needs to cut weight, and in doing so he often faces resistance from family and friends. These people usually have a hard enough time accepting a new rider's training and corollary lifestyle changes without having to accustom themselves to what one black humorist has called the Dachau look.

Ideal body types for endurance sports start at lean and progress to emaciation. When your sedentary aunt tells you that you look

A naturally hefty build needn't hold you back in cycling, so don't be discouraged if
you cannot achieve the rail-thin appearance of many top riders. Greg Demgen,
nicknamed Dough Boy, has become a very successful racer despite a body more
suited for a football lineman. Whatever your body type, a winter program of diet
and exercise will help pare off useless weight.

good, you are probably 10 pounds overweight. As a new rider it is tough to see yourself with the kind of lean body needed for top performance, and it is even tougher to withstand the well-meaning advice of friends and family who will feel that you are too thin for your own good. Remember that their frame of reference is overstuffed America. If you listen to the subjective and often prejudiced views of those around you, you will hear nothing but inaccurate and misleading estimates of what you should weigh. You are interested in making yourself very fit, not making sure your clothes still fit.

The second pitfall is the tendency of some riders to go overboard in search of what this or that expert says should be their perfect weight. This can be misleading because of differences among endurance sports. The very lean body composition of marathoners has become the goal of many cyclists simply because it is on runners that most of the testing has been done. But according to Dr. Ed Burke's study ("Too Fat? Testing of Top U.S. Riders Gives Guide" in *Inside the Cyclist*), the mean fat percentage of top-caliber American bike racers is about 8.5, quite a high figure when compared to elite runners, who have been reported as low as 2-3%.

Yet the more-muscular and longer-lasting demands of cycling seem to necessitate a more rugged body structure. Nowhere in running are the severe requirements of stage racing equalled. Perhaps very lean athletes can do well in one-day events, but they will tend to break down over a period of time. How many runners could be competitive in (or even finish) three or seven or 20 marathons on consecutive days? Yet cyclists are able to handle similar challenges. Interestingly, ultra-marathon runners tend to be stockier than their shorter-distance counterparts, perhaps because it takes a stronger system to absorb the punishment of 50- to 100-mile runs.

In a *Velo-news* interview, Greg LeMond commented on the Soviet riders that he and the U.S. team faced while competing in French stage races in the spring of 1980: "They look like turkeys. They've got hairy legs and some of them are a little fat. But they just go fast." Without a doubt the USSR is currently the top amateur cycling nation. Do they go fast because they are more concerned with having the strength to train hard than with some theoretical ideal body composition?

The quest for a perfect percentage of body fat can actually be destructive to a rider's training program and race performance. If you make sure that your workouts and diet are of high quality, you are usually safe letting the pounds take care of themselves. The architectural maxim — form follows function — is nowhere more important than in the search for the ideal competitive weight. However, if you suspect that you are too heavy, a body fat measurement is the best way to find out. Ignore the commonly used height/weight tables; they are useless because they give only statistical averages gleaned from insurance company files. They are an average for sedentary Americans and have no bearing on what an endurance athlete should weigh — except that it should be far less.

The important factor is body composition, not weight. For example, a 6-foot, 210-pound football player may be only 8% fat while a 6-foot, 160-pound sedentary office worker may have 20%. Ignore the scales except to record your weight before and after workouts, and use body fat percent to get an idea of your best race weight.

Body fat measurement can be done with a skinfold test or by underwater weighing. Both procedures are somewhat complex and require special equipment, but the skinfold measurement is within the means of most riders. Perhaps you could get it done at a local college, or your club could entice someone with calipers to come to a meeting and do all the members. In-shape male cyclists generally carry less than 10% body fat, women perhaps 5% more. Burke's previously mentioned article gives the actual readings for many of the country's best riders.

Reaching racing weight

Once you have determined your percent of fat, you can calculate your best competitive weight. Suppose you weigh 165 pounds and you test out at 14%. This means that about 23 pounds of your total weight is fat. Your fat-free weight, then, would be about 142 pounds. Since some body fat is necessary for fuel reserves, vitamin storage and padding around vital organs, you might want to shoot for 7%. This would mean reducing from your present 165 pounds to about 153, assuming that all weight lost is fat.

Remember that a program of diet *and* exercise is needed to ensure that fat loss is not accompanied by a reduction in muscle volume. If you cut calories too much and too fast, there will be insufficient energy to train properly. When the body's glycogen stores are depleted, it eventually turns to protein for energy. The source is the same muscle tissue that makes you go fast and which must be jealously guarded.

If the skinfold calipers, your performance and an objective look in the mirror all say that you are carrying too much fat, the actual process of losing it need not be as gruesome as often described. A pound of fat contains about 3,500 calories. If each day you decrease your calories by 500 and increase your mileage by 15, you will incur a 1,000-calorie deficit and drop two pounds a week. This is about the maximum that should be attempted in order to still have enough strength for training.

The off-season is the best time to undertake this program because hard training and racing demand a high calorie consumption to supply energy. The middle of the season is no time to go on a program of dietary restriction; the advantages of weight loss will be more than offset by reduced strength and vitality. Instead, plan to reach ideal weight during the winter so that when training begins in earnest you can devote your energy to getting the engine in tune rather than working on the chassis.

In fact, you don't even need to diet. Those 500 calories you want to cut each day can come out of items that add very little to your nutritional needs or dining satisfaction. If you have sugar in your coffee or tea, two tablespoons a day are worth 200 calories. If you eat your toast without honey or margarine, you save another 100. Drink water instead of a soft drink and save 120. Forget the salad dressing, don't eat that piece of candy or that donut and you have avoided 500 calories without pain.

One key to the program is knowing exactly how many calories you need each day to maintain your present weight. To find out, keep a tally of everything you eat for a week and figure the calorie content with the help of one of those little calorie counter booklets you find at supermarket checkouts. Be accurate — weigh and measure all servings. Then find your average daily intake. Weigh yourself before and after the test week, and if you have remained the same you know how many calories per day are required to maintain your present weight at current activity levels. You can then adjust your eating and training to produce the desired weight loss.

Continue to record your caloric consumption while you are reducing. In this way you can always tell exactly where you stand; it helps to know whether that piece of pie is safe to eat or if it will put you over your target calories for the day. This is also an important technique to keep from getting too inspired, eating too little, and as a result not having energy to train.

Once you are at your optimum weight and training hard, your diet will have to be modified to reflect the large number of calories being used. This modification seems to be towards sheer gluttony if some of the recent research as well as long-term observation is correct. Appetites of competitive cyclists have become legendary. The cafeteria staff at the college that houses riders for the Coors Classic is annually amazed at the average bikie's capacity. It was remarked that only football players came close.

Dr. David Costill, writing in the May, 1980, issue of *The Runner*, discussed research that indicates a direct relationship between the amount of food eaten and the amount of glycogen stored in the muscles. The more grams of carbohydrate you pack in, the more glycogen will be available to fuel your on-bike efforts.

It also appears that the cyclist riding 200 or more hard miles per week can eat large amounts, including junk food and pastry, without gaining weight. This seems to be the case even when caloric consumption is greater than energy expenditure. Several reasons are offered for this phenomenon: (1) The athlete who exercises daily burns the glycogen from the previous day's eating before it can be converted to fat; (2) The body's metabolism is raised by exercise and the increased use of calories continues after each day's ride; (3) Athletes are active people who burn more energy at everyday tasks than ordinary people — they will run up a flight of stairs rather than walk, for instance. It all means that once you have reached a weight where you are effective on the bike and in everyday activities, don't try to go lower in hopes of improving performance still more. The odds are almost totally against it.

Reaching your best competitive weight is just like any other part of your cycling program. It requires some careful thought, a little dedication and a moderate approach.

9
Injuries
Recovery can often be hastened
by an aggressive, positive attitude

IT IS EVERY cyclist's fate to get injured. Sometime in your career it will happen, whether due to a crash, overuse or a biomechanical problem. Certain riders seem to have the amazing ability to take these interruptions in stride and return to peak form rapidly. Others are mentally destroyed and lose weeks, whole seasons, or even give up the bike in disgust.

You must develop the ability to overcome injuries or your racing career — to say nothing of your general fitness and health — will be doomed. To borrow a phrase from the heavy equipment industry, you have to avoid "down time." The more down time a trucker experiences while his rig is being repaired, the less money he makes. Similarly, if your body is always in the repair shop you will lose fitness. And while a truck can operate at full strength immediately after being repaired, the human body must rebuild gradually to return to its former efficiency.

About half the questions I receive from riders in response to my writing in *Velo-news* are about injuries, and the vast majority concern knee problems. I sympathize. I know of no injury, with the possible exception of chronic fatigue from overtraining, that is so depressing and frustrating. Fractures heal and head injuries usually kill you outright (eliminating the problems of recovery) but chronic knee pain alternately quiets down and flares up, disrupting training for a long time as it slowly saps the desire to ride. Because of this, my following comments about recovering from injuries will be aimed specifically at knees, but they are applicable to most other serious physical problems that cyclists face. In the next chapter I will give some advice for dealing with the less traumatic problems of road rash, numbness and saddle sores.

I have had my share of knee miseries, including the usual football damage in college, tendinitis from cycling and chondromalacia from running. From this experience and from conversations with athletes, doctors and trainers, I offer these guidelines:

There are no universal cures. Some injuries respond to rest while others can be ridden through. Some feel better after 10 miles; others get progressively worse, even making it difficult to simply turn around and ride back home. Variations in pedaling style, riding position and biomechanical efficiency virtually assure that each knee injury will occur in a slightly different way for every rider. As a result different cures are necessary, but my general rule has always been to avoid layoffs of more than a day or two if at all possible. Many athletes have experienced the phenomenon of ceasing activity for a month and having their injury occur again immediately upon resumption of training. The body doesn't know you want it to get well unless you ask it to. Let pain be your guide to what you are able to do without making the injury more serious.

Doctors are usually of little help. Most conventional physicians are helpful only if an injury is the result of trauma. If they can see swelling, diagnose torn cartilage or x-ray a broken bone, they can operate or prescribe appropriate treatment. For the more subtle overuse injuries commonly associated with cycling, most doctors know less than you do — and the good ones will admit it. The exception is the new breed of sportsmedicine physicians — the so-called jock docs — who have personal experience with their own injuries and professional experience with those of other athletes. But they are hard to find and nearly impossible to see in time for treatment before the race next weekend.

You must be responsible for your own cure. You are your own best doctor in most cases. The medical establishment can work near-miracles with antibiotics, disease detection devices like the CAT scanner, and reconstructive surgery. However, it usually falls flat when subtle injuries are involved. Because of this you have to try various approaches on yourself. It all comes down to knowing your own body. Experience helps, of course. Most injuries cyclists suffer tend to be recurring, so if you ride long enough you will get the opportunity to try out various cures.

Self treatment

What do you do when your knee (or ankle or Achilles tendon) starts hurting? First, treat it with a short rest, ice and aspirin. If it begins to hurt during a training ride, don't grind away another 50 miles or you will only be opening yourself to worse injury and a longer recovery period. Most suspicious twinges will vanish after a day or so of rest if you respond to them early in their development.

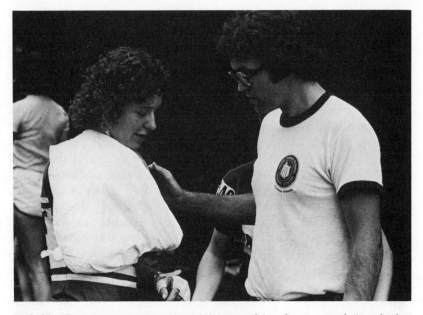

Probably the most common serious injury resulting from a crash is a broken collarbone. Consoling this stricken rider is Ed Burke, a Ph.D. in exercise physiology who has become a well-known figure in U.S. cycling. While technical director for the U.S. Cycling Federation he worked with national team members at the Olympic Training Center in Colorado Springs and also helped hold clinics around the country for the rank-and-file competitor. He has written several books and many articles for cycling magazines. Burke agrees that a key to quick recovery from an injury is to stay as active as possible and adopt a positive mental attitude.

You have to have the experience to know which pains can be ridden through and which are harbingers of trouble. One rule of thumb says that if pain subsides while riding, ride. But when it worsens while riding it's best to halt the workout.

If the pain persists after a day off, continue taking aspirin to reduce inflammation. Aspirin, doctors assure me, is a safe drug. I don't like to take any medicine, but I will take aspirin when I'm hurt so I can resume riding sooner. It seems to help.

Hasten recovery by using ice or heat on the injured part. Ice is the new panacea, recommended by trainers and physicians as the answer to most athletic injuries that have traditionally been treated in a hot whirlpool. However, the use of heat shouldn't be relegated to the medical trash heap. The time it should definitely not be used is in the early stages of an injury where tissue has been severely damaged. In this case heat will only increase the swelling, but ice will keep it to a minimum. So will elevation of the injured part, if that's possible.

A friend of mine swears by heat for his infrequent knee problems. At the first sign of trouble he sleeps with a heating pad wrapped around the afflicted knee and wears a hot pack bandaged in place during the day. Three days of this around-the-clock blitz is enough, he claims, to cure the most stubborn case of tendinitis. But because it works for him doesn't necessarily mean it will for you. Experiment.

Don't let yourself get out of shape and overweight during treatment. These are depressing times because you are forced to decrease your training in both quantity and intensity, perhaps for an extended period. If you continue to eat a 300-mile-a-week diet you will gain weight steadily and rapidly after about the first week of inactivity. This is bad enough, but many cyclists also get depressed when they can't ride and some personalities are so constructed that their response is a bad case of the munchies. An injured, depressed athlete who overeats will look like the Hindenburg in short order. Solutions:

Cut back on calories. While you are injured is actually a good time to lose weight because the weakness caused by dieting won't matter if you can't train anyway. Mentally, it is a positive move because you will feel you are doing something to benefit your future performance despite the layoff.

Try to stay physically fit. A knee injured by pedaling a bike may still allow you to swim or do some other aerobic activity like cross-country skiing or walking without pain. If nothing else, at least lift weights for the upper body and do abdominal exercises. One rider who broke his collarbone walked fast 10 miles a day until he could get back on the bike. It hurt and it took time but he didn't lose much fitness. Also, he didn't gain an ounce because walking burns about 100 calories a mile.

Realize that it takes work to get well. Be regular and disciplined in your treatment. Don't neglect to take aspirin, use ice and/or do your rehabilitative exercises. Injuries heal by themselves, but they heal faster if you put physical and mental energy into the cure.

All these techniques for fighting injuries come down to your mental attitude. If you get depressed, if you doubt that you will ever heal, if you cling to a doctor's every word, chances are that your recovery will be long and arduous. If you adopt an aggressive but realistic stance toward your plight and face the injury directly with the attitude that no misfortune can get you down, you will be back on the bike soon. The impetus for recovery comes ultimately from your own body and mental state.

10
Road Hazards
Coping with a world of perils from bad dogs to saddle sores

CYCLISTS EXIST in a constantly changing environment. Every new mile of road that passes under our wheels presents its own set of challenges and, let's be honest, hazards. Football players don't have to share the practice field with 55-m.p.h. traffic nor are basketball courts full of potholes and glass, but the serious cyclist must train daily in the presence of these and various other potential dangers. Therefore, concentration is required not only on the skills of the sport but on everything in the world around. Before launching into the sections on training and racing, here is a look at how to deal with a number of common cycling roadblocks — both environmental and physical — which you are likely to encounter.

Dogs and other animals
The dog dilemma is highly publicized in cycling literature but perhaps overrated. It is really a people problem; pets need to be restrained and leash laws must be enforced.

Beginning riders tend to load their bikes with chemical sprays, rocks to throw and high-frequency alarms, then learn by experience that dogs are rarely enough of a hassle to warrant such an arsenal. When you are threatened by a dog, simple tactics work best. I am not particularly afraid of being bitten but I do dread the overzealous canine that dashes out of nowhere and takes me down. The key to successful defense is keeping the animal out of the front wheel, something made a little easier by a dog's natural tendency to attack from the rear flank. A friend once had a dog hit his rear wheel hard enough to skid it several inches to the side (the mutt ran out hard and apparently lost traction on the pavement) but there was no loss of bike control. However, even minor contact with the front wheel, let alone a wallop like that, can be disastrous.

I find that the best strategy when I'm confronted is to raise my hand threateningly as if I have a rock. Nearly every dog understands that gesture and will slow down at least momentarily. It often helps to accompany that bluff with the commands "No! Stay!" in as loud and authoritative a voice as can be mustered. You are looking to buy enough time to get out of the dog's well-defined and rather small domain. Once the territorial boundry is reached, a ferocious defender of the turf will often instantly turn into a harmless barker.

In cases where an aggressive dog and poor timing work in concert, you may have to get off the bike. An example is a big dog that comes snarling after you while you are going uphill. You can't outrun him, so dismount and use your bike as a shield. If you need to, throw rocks picked up from the side of the road or use your pump as a club. Some riders have reported success with the widely available chemical sprays, but the wind makes accuracy a problem and you may be risking a crash if you try to spray a charging dog while moving down the road. To help prevent a loss of control, always grip the bars on top right next to the stem when taking the other hand away. In this position you will be much less likely to jerk the front wheel during any flailing around.

If a dog is a persistent hazard on a favorite training route, it pays to locate the owner and tell him of the problem. Be courteous but firm about the necessity of controlling his pet. Resort to legal threats only when diplomacy and reason fail. The law should be on your side — you have a right to use public roads free of being attacked.

Dogs aren't the only animals you might encounter and others can be just as dangerous. For example:

— On a training ride once I was almost cooked by a large, angry and hissing goose.

— The course for the annual Denver City Park Criterium goes around a lake and one year 30 of us in a tight bunch swept through a corner to be confronted by a whole flock of ducks waddling slowly across the road. Disaster was averted by the alert bike handling of the riders and the unexpected agility of the ducks.

— In the Milk Race, several riders, including the Polish star Szurkowski, were taken down by a flock of sheep who were spooked by the riders on one of Britain's back roads.

— In Colorado, ranchers use public roads to move large herds of cows to high pastures in the spring and back again in the fall. This may be picturesque and smack of Old West nostalgia, but riding through 200 cows is a slow and messy process.

Squirrels are a problem, too. Not the two-legged variety you see in bike races but the wild, four-legged, nut-storing kind. Like small dogs they have a disturbing tendency to shoot across the road in front of you, bushy tail flying, with no warning at all. Usually you won't crash if you hit one, but their erratic dashes can be unnerving. Watch out for an instant about-face just when you think they are out of the way.

I am still not sure that the most exotic road hazard in my local bestiary ever really existed. I was on a long, fast, solo training ride on the back roads of southwestern Colorado. It was hot and I was pushing hard on the hills as well as doing one-mile, all-out efforts every 10 miles or so. I was light-headed from the exertion and from a month of reduced caloric intake in an attempt to get my body fat below 8%. As I sat up after a jam, eyes misty with perspiration and vision blurred from fatigue and effort, a large peacock ran into the road in front of me and stopped, multicolored tail feathers spread in all their shimmering glory. I braked abruptly and swerved to the left. When I looked back the road was empty. I shook my head, wiped my eyes and vowed to eat more — I was obviously hallucinating from exertion and the bonk. Colorado has a definite shortage of wild peacocks and there wasn't a zoo in sight.

I hadn't pedaled another 100 yards when I rounded a corner and came face to face with a full-grown male buffalo, shaggy mane billowing as he clattered off the road and up an embankment. That was it, the absolute last straw. I turned around and pedaled slowly and carefully back home and ate a big dinner. I have driven and ridden that road many times since then and have discovered that the buffalo does exist (a local rancher owns him) but I've never spotted the peacock. Given the state of my blood sugar that day, little green men from Mars were entirely possible. Some road hazards are more internal than external.

Railroad tracks and obstacles

Railroad tracks always pose a danger. On training rides they should be dealt with conservatively by slowing down, getting out of the saddle and using the handlebars to lift the front wheel slightly an instant before contact. It isn't necessary to actually jump the bike over the tracks as racers will often do when there is just one set. Simply time it so that most of your weight is floating on the pedals when contact is made, thus reducing the chance of tire and rim damage.

Tracks that run diagonally to the road are especially hazardous and should be taken at right angle if possible. Otherwise they

Jumping is a useful skill to avoid obstacles, not just in cyclocross or mountain bike races but in road training and racing. Practice on a grassy field, using your second-best bike.

could catch and twist your front wheel, resulting in especially bad damage to both you and the bike. Remember that when rails, metal bridge surfaces, sewer grates, etc. are wet they are even slipperier than the pavement.

Good bike handlers sometimes prefer to jump over small

obstacles. I was training once with experienced Boulder riders Tom Mereness and Mike Nettles on roads unfamiliar to me. Tom was pulling hard and I was behind him when he turned and yelled something back that I didn't understand. At the same time I saw the sign for a railroad track. Abruptly, Tom got out of the saddle and sprinted. Not wanting to be left behind, and assuming that he had yelled back to tell me we were going to do an interval or something, I got on his wheel. When we reached the tracks he soared neatly over them, gazelle-like, right in front of me. In the space below his wheels I could see those glinting steel rails sticking up two inches from the patched blacktop. I had just enough time to pull up on the bars and avoid a crash. It turned out that Tom had shouted "Bad tracks coming up!" and had accelerated to get the momentum needed to jump them. Mike, who knew the road and was used to Tom's acrobatic riding style, had slowed down and was watching my reaction, and my fate, with keen enjoyment.

The ability to jump the bike is useful and can be learned easily; after all, every BMX kid can hurdle over curbs with ease. Practice on a smooth, grassy field using your second-best bike. The penalties for a mistake are not as pronounced if you fall on grass. Pull evenly on the drop part of the bars with your hands and pull up on the pedals at the same time. It is just a matter of coordination.

Another time that jumping the bike comes in handy is when you find yourself on the shoulder of the road. Should you try to ride directly back onto the pavement the raised edge will deflect your front wheel and take you down. Instead, do as Boulder racer Bob Ware did in the Franktown race some years ago when he was elbowed off the road. He stayed parallel to the edge for a short distance and then jumped the bike up and sideways, landing neatly on the pavement with scarcely a wobble. This simple bike-handling skill transformed a potentially disastrous situation into a minor incident.

Slippery surfaces

Gravel or sand in corners can cause a skid and a spill. When training, corner with some caution unless you are sure the road surface is clean. It can vary from day to day as rain and traffic litter the road with debris that wasn't there the last time you took the route. In races, corners are supposed to be swept clean but this is not always done or done well. A stable bike with good tires can be skidded slightly in a little loose gravel without loss of control.

Cornering on wet roads is risky business. When training, take it easy and perhaps pedal all the way through to keep yourself from heeling the bike over too far. When racing, keep your weight back and stand hard on that outside pedal. Staying upright takes good judgment, experience . . . and some luck.

Keep your weight back on the rear wheel and avoid abrupt moves — heel the bike over smoothly and let it find its own line through the corner. Don't fight the bike. The same goes when riding straight through any loose surface. Sit on the back of the saddle and use a higher gear than normal so you can push on through. Keep a light touch on the bars.

Damp roads are slippery and unpredictable no matter the source of the moisture. Rain often makes roads most treacherous just after it begins and causes oil and dirt to float up; in a few minutes traction generally improves. Cornering on wet pavement requires the same technique as on gravel — smooth and steady is the key. Some riders advocate pedaling through the turn instead of coasting with the outside pedal down. I suspect that this works because you can't bank the bike over as far, which ensures more tire adhesion. Another trick is to reduce air pressure slightly in wet weather so that more tread is in contact with the road.

A less frequently encountered hazard is a layer of fallen leaves. They tend to be as slippery as the worst oil slick and far less obvious. Be careful in the fall — or you will.

Motor vehicles

The greatest road hazard is motor vehicles. As a bicycle rider you are exposing your unprotected mortal flesh in terrain that belongs to massive monsters of steel and glass. The best way to stay alive is to obey traffic laws and ride defensively. Cyclists have a bad reputation, in part deserved, for running red lights, stop signs and in general paying scant attention to traffic laws. This is a great way to eventually get seriously hurt.

Cyclists aren't always at fault, however. Motorists have a peculiar blind spot when it comes to bicycles. Maybe it's because a bike and rider make a relatively small, inconspicuous object. I theorize that drivers are used to kids' bikes going 5 m.p.h. and that's why they will often pull out right in front of a cyclist training at 25. In any case, wear bright colors, wear a helmet and be always alert. Riding with your head down is a sure way to get nailed.

Harassment by drivers indicates part of the sickness of the human race: We persecute individuals we perceive as different from ourselves. As a cyclist you may be verbally derided or blatantly attacked. Mace, martial arts and training in groups for protection are possible answers, but they don't solve the problem of the drunk driver who runs you off the road, or the truck driver who has to prove his masculinity by seeing how close he can bring his rig to your left elbow. There is no easy solution to the danger posed by such deviant behavior. Like any aspect of life, it is something that must be accepted as part of the game. Such harassment can be minimized if you go about your business in a safe, defensive, law-abiding way and avoid flashy or attention-producing behavior. If you have a choice, stay off heavily traveled roads. In some locales it might be just as wise to avoid those that are quiet and lonely.

Fellow riders

Fellow cyclists are a threat to your safety. In races or when training in a group you are at the mercy of others. Again, defensive riding is a must. Never overlap someone's rear wheel assuming that he will ride a straight line. Watch for poor bike handlers and give them enough room so that they won't include you in their mistakes. The front third of the pack is the safest place because there are fewer riders to balk your strategic moves or to do things that can take you down.

Riders at the front should point to potholes, glass and other hazards so those behind whose vision is obscured can avoid them. Don't yell "Glass!" or "Hole!" as this only wastes breath and creates confusion if it isn't heard clearly. A gesture is sufficient communication. Point down with the left hand if you intend to go by with the hazard on the left, and vice versa.

Above all, help poor bike handlers with constructive criticism. Nothing is more disheartening to the aspiring novice than to be yelled at and insulted for a lack of ability. Once you have gained some experience, try to make low-key and useful suggestions to those less skilled. If you are a new rider, accept these corrections gracefully if offered and find other people to ride with if they aren't. The sport doesn't need and can ill afford the kind of obnoxious elitism sometimes shown by experienced racers toward rookies.

Punctures

You can keep flats to a minimum by brushing off the tread with your hand immediately after running over anything suspicious. Most punctures don't happen instantly but are the result of something being picked up by a tire and then ground in during the next few revolutions. Make it a habit to brush your fingertips across the spinning tires every few minutes, but when doing the rear be careful to not let your hand get jammed between the wheel and the frame. You could wind up doing a cartwheel. Let the back of your hand slide down the seat tube and then extend one or two fingers to the tire. Before long you will learn the exact position of the wheel and be able to reach directly to it.

While punctures and cut casings are inevitable, the risk can be lowered by avoiding overinflation. Rock-hard tires feel fast and efficient but they cannot absorb the broken pavement and bits of debris that would normally cause no damage. On the other hand, underinflation can lead to weakened sidewalls and blowouts.

When a puncture occurs, keep your weight back and come to a stop using steady pressure on the brakes. If you're in a racing pack, raise an arm once you have your bike under control. This lets others know exactly where that bang came from and helps them give you clearance. If there is a wheel van behind, throw up the left arm for a front flat, the right for a rear. This corresponds with which shift lever controls which derailleur (front/rear) and allows the mechanic to have the correct wheel at the ready.

Broken spokes are another common wheel problem. If one snaps at any time other than in a race, the best thing to do is stop immediately and unscrew it from the nipple. It can't do you any good in the wheel and it could do a lot of harm, particularly if is under the freewheel and it snags the derailleur the next time you shift into low gear. One broken spoke shouldn't put the wheel so far out of true that you can't complete the ride, but take it easy. When you get home and put in the replacement, simply tighten it to the same tension as its neighbors and the wheel should go right back in true. If you constantly break spokes it is a tip-off that you are too heavy for the wheels or there is a bad match between the diameters of the spokes and the holes in the hub flange.

Crashing and its aftermath

In spite of everything you do to avoid it, you will crash sooner or later. In fact, probably sooner than later. Most solo accidents take place during the first season of serious cycling as riders are just beginning to develop the experience and reflexes necessary to stay upright under varying conditions. As you accumulate hours in the saddle you will develop a sort of sixth sense of danger, the ability to feel potentially hazardous situations before they fully develop. Most crashes are relatively minor affairs. If you have a choice, try to slide rather than tumble. Damage confined to one side is painful enough, but at least you will have an uninjured side to sleep on. Tumbling falls almost guarantee that no sitting or reclining position will be comfortable, and they increase the chance of broken collarbones and arms as your extremities fly around.

Intentionally or not, Steve Tilford has reacted correctly to his predicament. As pro rider Jonathan Boyer advises, when a crash is happening "the first thing you want to do is to get away from your bike. Let go of the bars and land flat on your hands and stomach. If you hold onto the bars, you go onto your collarbone. If you watch the big European sprinters, the man goes down flat and his bike is behind him."

Some people advocate protecting your head by clutching it with both arms when you hit. However, you will rarely have time to react that quickly and if you are wearing a hardshell helmet it is unnecessary.

If you do get an abrasion — "road rash" as it is colorfully called — treatment is simple. Wash the wound carefully with soap or medicated cleanser. Be sure to get out all road grime, pieces of gravel and other foreign objects — use a brush if necessary. Shaved legs are unquestionably an advantage here. Then coat the abrasion with antibiotic salve. Use a non-stick dressing when you must cover it, but healing will be quickened by exposure to air. A scab is undesirable because it will reduce range of motion and then crack open during riding, so keep the wound moist with salve. A tetanus antitoxin shot is recommended within the first 24 hours if you haven't had one in the last couple of years.

Be sure to carefully monitor the healing of road rash. At the first signs of infection — redness, swelling, fever — see a doctor. Cuts and abrasions that don't heal may be a sign of lowered resistance brought on by overtraining or serious problems like diabetes. In case of suspected bone or joint damage, excessive swelling, puncture wounds, deep cuts or any head injury, forget the home remedy and get professional medical attention.

One way to keep upper body abrasions to a minimum is to wear a light cotton or polypro T-shirt under the jersey. In the event of a crash the outer garment will slide against the inner one instead of your skin, leaving considerably less road rash. I recommend wearing an undershirt during racing and group training, the times when you are most likely to be involved in a spill due to the presence of other riders.

Saddle sores

The bane of the serious cyclist is the chafing that leads to saddle sores. These lesions are caused when the bacteria which are always present on the skin enter minute breaks that result during thousands of pedal strokes. The ultimate condition is infected hair follicles and the formation of pustules. The experience of having a boil lanced *down there* will literally curl your toes. It needn't ever come to that, however.

While the lore of the European sport includes tales of riders so afflicted by saddle sores that they had to ride entire races standing up — the great Eddy Merckx's never-ending search for saddle comfort is well documented — most of us don't ride anywhere near the mileage of the pros nor must we stay on the bike at all costs to make a living. Still, saddle sores can be a dispiriting and frustrating problem. It pays to do everything possible to prevent them or at least minimize their impact on daily riding.

Cleanliness is of primary importance, followed by proper equipment and bike setup. Thoroughly clean the crotch with rubbing alcohol before and after every ride. This will kill bacteria and it seems to toughen the skin. Don't stay in your cycling shorts for longer than necessary after riding. Have at least two shorts so that you will always have a clean pair to wear. Wash them right after riding and hang them outside to dry; it is suspected that the ultraviolet rays in sunlight help kill the bacteria. Before wearing the shorts again, rub up the chamois and apply a lubricant to make it soft and flexible. Many riders like a water-based substance such as Noxema because it is easy to wash out. Other prefer petroleum jelly, A-and-D Ointment, Kucharik's Chamois Fat, etc.

Some go for baby powder and a few prefer nothing at all. Experiment to find out what suits you best. Only buy shorts that contain a large, thick, soft chamois which has no protruding seams. Just as importantly, the shorts should fit so that the legs stay down instead of bunching up in the crotch, which will contribute to chafing.

Correct saddle location (discussed in chapter 2) is also important in the battle against crotch problems. If the saddle is too high or too low the resulting rocking or bouncing during pedaling will quickly abrade the skin and contribute to bruising. If the tilt is wrong your constant sliding in and out of position will multiply the normal friction.

If in spite of doing everything right your crotch does become raw, tender and small sores begin to appear, don't despair. It is probably safe to say that everyone who trains daily for fitness and racing has at least a minor condition. It should be entirely manageable as long as you continue with good hygiene. However, if things do get out of hand your pharmacist or doctor can recommend a medication to use in the chamois and/or after riding.

Numbness

Loss of sensation in the hands, feet and crotch is uncomfortable and upsetting. Fortunately, it's not hard to prevent. Numbness is caused by compression of nerves and blood vessels, as might be guessed from the fact that the parts involved are the contact points between the body and the bike.

Hands are perhaps most commonly affected. Sensation usually returns quickly, but there are reports of riders suffering from numb fingers for days or even weeks. One key to prevention is wearing cycling gloves with a padded palm and/or using one of the various padded handlebar wraps on the market. Even more important, though, is developing the habit of changing hand position every few minutes. By going from the tops to the hoods to the drops and back again you will prevent the uniform pressure that puts hands to sleep. An added benefit of this frequent movement is the changes it creates in upper body position. This is important for fending off muscle fatigue and tightness in the neck, shoulders, arms and lower back.

You will sometimes see a rider squirting water on his feet in an attempt to put out a fire that isn't really there. Hot-feeling or numb feet occur when blood circulation is reduced. This can be caused by shoes or toe straps that are too tight, but a more common reason is the constant pressure on the bottom of the feet.

Most cycling shoes have no insole or only a piece of leather, which is not sufficient padding. After inserting a pair of resilient insoles, such as those that Spenco makes, the problem should disappear. You can also try wearing thicker socks. Of course, if you are riding in running shoes or a catch-all model made for cycling and walking, there will not be adequate protection against the pressure of the pedal. Besides feeling uncomfortable, you won't be able to transmit your power as fully or efficiently as you would in cleated shoes with a rigid sole.

You may not fully understand what panic is until the first time your crotch goes numb. At any rate, you won't want it to happen again. It is usually preventable, though you may find that it occurs to some extent after making lengthy, hard efforts in a low riding position, such as when time trialing. The reason then is the pressure caused by the nose of the saddle. Otherwise, crotch numbness can be prevented by wearing shorts with a thick chamois, by using a correctly positioned saddle containing a layer of dense foam, and by frequently altering sitting position. Ride on the back of the saddle, in the center and towards the nose, and stand up for a few pedal strokes occasionally to relieve pressure. As with the upper body, you have to cultivate the habit of moving around on the bike to relieve pressure points and delay fatigue.

PART III

Training

11
Principles
of Training
*Self-knowledge is the key
to an optimum cycling program*

TRAINING FOR BIKE RACING can be enormously confusing for the newcomer because of the widely different theories. The LSD advocates preach miles and miles at a steady aerobic pace to build endurance, expand cardiovascular capacity and energize the psycho-endocrine system for the stresses of racing. Others argue that because bike races proceed at an uneven pace, ranging from merely cruising to guts-on-the-road jams, LSD is virtually useless. They favor speed training like intervals, hard time trials and hill work.

In the barrage of conflicting claims and strident advice, the experienced competitor can be as confused as the novice. He may have raced for several years, but in the attempt to continue his improvement he can easily fall prey to gnawing doubt and insecurity about his supposedly time-tested methods.

In spite of all the opinions, however, there are some general principles of training that hold true regardless of the specific methods employed. If you base your training pattern on these proven fundamentals, you are not likely to go wrong with whichever specific techniques you choose.

Stress adaptation

All training is based on the stress adaptation system of the body. In a process known as the general adaptation syndrome, the body reacts to stress by becoming stronger. When a stress such as training is applied, the body becomes better able to cope with that stress. If the training is not severe enough, improvement does not take place or it proceeds at a slow rate. But if the stress is too severe, or if insufficient time is allowed for recovery between training sessions, the body will break down instead of becoming stronger. The proper training load, then, is a two-edged sword — the cutting edge aims in two directions and only the middle holds the promise of safety and success.

For the racer, the application of this principle is easy in theory. All you have to do is work the body enough in training to make it adapt and grow stronger. Maximum improvement is achieved by treading that fine line between too much stress and too little.

In practice, however, this is incredibly difficult to do for several reasons. In the first place, we don't know for sure how much stress is needed to produce optimum results. It varies not only from one individual to another but also within each person, depending on age, degree of fitness and current mental state. No empirical guideline can be given.

Sport physiologists are currently experimenting with various tests to determine an individual's optimum training load. The most publicized involves sampling blood from the earlobe during workouts and monitoring various components — lactate levels, for instance — to set up a scientific guide to training. However, such procedures are still not proven and are unwieldly even for national-class racers with access to labs and a bevy of doctors. The rest of us can forget it. This is why training plans that prescribe intervals by the dose (such as 10 repetitions of two minutes on, two minutes off) are so useless. You have to learn to read your own body's reactions to training and decide what you need on each particular day. It may very well be those 10 intervals. On the other hand, it may be a one-hour nap.

And training is not the only stress to which the racing cyclist is exposed. Your job, schoolwork and family, plus factors like not getting enough sleep, add to the total stress you experience. One week a training session of 10 intervals may be the perfect amount of work for improvement; the next week you may be spending late nights at work, eating badly and worrying about it all, making the same 10 intervals destructive when combined with the additional stress. In fact, non-national-class riders are often more susceptible to stress overloads than those who have only their bike racing to consider. Those who must shoehorn training around a family and job or heavy academic load have to be especially careful.

As much as the scientific community would like to devise ways to tell us exactly how much training to do at any given time, and as much as we would welcome such certainty, training at present is more art than science, more intuition than reason. We each have to learn through experience to judge what our bodies need.

Specificity

Training must resemble the activity you are preparing for. A freestyle swimmer becomes better by swimming freestyle, a hitter improves by taking batting practice, and a cyclist should devote the majority of his training time to riding. Running, skiing or riding the rollers may help your overall fitness, but it is getting out on the bike that will do the most to make you a better road racer. The more specific the training, the more closely the resulting adaptation translates into improved performance.

However, this principle has another and oft-overlooked facet: variety. Sometimes an activity, like cycling, has a number of different components and these can be worked on separately to achieve overall improvement. For instance, because bike races contain jams, sprints, hills and chases, part of the training should concentrate specifically on the development of speed. On the other hand, racing requires long-haul endurance and this makes LSD rides essential, too.

This specificity can be taken even farther. Weight training is not cycling, but it can improve cycling by stimulating important muscle groups. A half-squat, for instance, is very specific to cycling because it intensely works the quadriceps which are so involved in pedaling strength.

Variety is also a mental necessity. A steady diet of one training technique, no matter how much you enjoy it or believe in it, soon becomes unpalatable. Specificity and variety are not mutually exclusive in practice, although at first glance they might seem to be.

Systematic progress

The stress load should be increased as you grow stronger. This is true both for short and long-term considerations. Ideally, interval intensity and distances ridden should be increased during the season's build-up as you develop strength and endurance. If this is done with consideration for the total stress load, the improvement will theoretically be steady. Of course, this isn't how it actually works. Everyone has physiological limits and a graph of progress is often a series of rises and plateaus rather than a smoothly ascending curve. But the principle is still sound and it holds true even on a year-to-year basis; you should be able to do more each year if training is carefully planned. For example, at his 1985 training camp Greg LeMond stated that he had increased his mileage about 1,500 miles a year during the first three or four

Eric Heiden used his understanding of physiology, training, and how his body reacts to stress to quickly become a national-class cyclist following his speedskating success in the 1980 Winter Olympics. Since then he has alternated pre-med studies with racing, including an entry in the 1986 Tour de France. Heiden, by the way, found that in terms of cycling performance his great muscle mass put extra requirements on his circulatory system, so since his skating days he has allowed the loss of some upper body muscularity.

seasons of his career. He knows the secret of a moderate, steady increase in the training load to improve and reach long-term goals.

We are all unique both in our genetically inherited abilities and in the daily stresses we encounter. If there is one requisite of athletic training it is to be able to recognize this fact and plan workouts accordingly. We need to resist all shortcuts, miracle training plans and the highly publicized schedules of top riders. The best training plan for you is the one that works best for you. Only experience and self-analysis can produce an efficient program.

There is nothing more self-defeating than to do well in a race, shattering your best time or placing, but to have set your goals so high that you are more disheartened than satisfied. Those of us without a full-time commitment to racing should be careful when setting goals because we may not have the natural talent to attain them on restricted training. Everyone would like to ride a 25-mile time trial in 56 minutes or win a major race, but we also have families, jobs and responsibilities as well as the understanding that there is more to life than bike racing. This realization presents no problem if our priorities and goals reflect it.

Self-discipline

Self-discipline is a key aspect of training, but one usually viewed incorrectly by the casual participant or the layman. They tend to think that an athlete's race performance is the result of an iron will that drives him to suffer more in training. This is not true. Motivation supplies will power automatically. If you really want to race, the desire to train properly and arrange your life in the most effective way will rise naturally out of that goal. If you find it necessary to force yourself to do some part of your training, examine your motivation.

Every article on training lists the symptoms of overtraining and warns the athlete to beware of the signs and heed their warning. Yet it seems that every racer I have ever talked to has had bouts with deep-seated fatigue caused by forays over that metaphorical line separating productive training from overwork and breakdown. The key is that paradoxical form of self-discipline, which is to not drive yourself through pain and agony but rather to take a day off or go easy when needed.

Regardless of what coaches, teachers or other moral leaders of our society say when exhorting their charges to greater effort, it is easy to work too hard. It requires no thought, foresight or restraint. All you have to do is go out and hammer away every day. Nearly every self-coached and self-motivated rider does it sometime in his career. Certainly it is difficult to resist the guilt and compulsion that often forces us to follow some arbitrary schedule or preconceived notion of how many miles we need. But we must trust our unique and personal perceptions of how we feel.

Witness the following scenario, a situation all too common among highly motivated riders:

He has a good race so continues training with sky-rocketing enthusiasm. Hard intervals Monday, LSD Tuesday, a long time trial Wednesday, more speed work Thursday. He plans to taper down on Friday but gets caught up in the aura of big miles and high intensity. The scheduled easy workout becomes too long or too fast. At the race on Saturday he is physically tired but doesn't realize that this is why he does poorly. The enthusiasm of the week before now turns to discouragement, but to him the answer is obvious: more work. The next day he is back at it with the grim determination born of failure.

And so the cycle of fatigue, defeat and overtraining begins. The real solution is to temper enthusiasm, knowing that the quality and quantity of training is only half the equation that equals success. The other half is the rest that enables recovery and improvement.

Signals of overtraining

There is one "scientific" method that most experts use to spot and avoid the onset of overtraining: pulse rate monitoring. You do it by taking your resting pulse each day as you wake and are lying quietly in bed. Then take it again a few minutes after rising (the exact interval is not as important as being consistent from day to day). Record the figures and the difference between them for comparisons during the season as well as year to year. What you are looking for is an increase in either the resting rate or the difference, as this is supposed to signal caution. But at the risk of committing grave heresy, I must say that I find this technique of little practical value. In my case it tends to give misleading or inconsistent results. During one of the worst bouts of overtraining fatigue I've ever had, my resting pulse was consistently lower by nearly 10 beats a minute. It was as if my pulse was trying to tell me that I was in the process of killing myself. At other times it has gone up 10 beats over normal with no appreciable performance changes.

Also, pulse readings tend to be redundant. I know that I am overtrained and in need of rest by merely paying attention to several general symptoms. Of all the signs commonly listed, I find the following to be the most useful:

•A general feeling of fatigue that lingers from one day and one workout to the next.

•Tired legs that persist after the usual recovery time. They ache, feel heavy when climbing stairs, and throb when I am trying to go to sleep.

•Lowered pace of life. Sometimes I find myself bogging down in everyday activities. I walk more slowly and speak with less animation. It is as if my body has shut down the reactors slightly to conserve the energy needed to survive what I am doing to it. This is a dangerous sign because when a racer doesn't have sufficient energy for the usual business of living, it is a cinch he won't have enough for adaptation and improvement.

•Sleep irregularities. Dr. George Sheehan calls it "depression insomnia," characterized by ease in falling asleep in the evening but inability to remain asleep. The overtrained rider often wakes in the wee hours, his mind racing like a flywheel out of control, unable to relax. Then at about 10 o'clock the next morning, he is ready for a nap. For me, this feeling of being out of synch with my usual schedule and the world in general is the most obvious signal of too much work.

A word of caution: These and similar symptoms can be vague and are seldom dramatic. They begin innocently and increase in intensity gradually, and you may experience different symptoms than the ones that affect me. Unfortunately, the only way to discover how your body reacts to overtraining is to occasionally push farther than normal and see what happens. Human nature being what it is, the enthusiastic beginning rider and the more experienced racer eager for improvement are bound to create their opportunities.

All these principles must be viewed holistically and combined wisely when you structure a personal training program. Ignoring any one of them can lead to slowed improvement or more severe problems. Optimum training is not based on haphazard riding but is the result of thought, knowledge, moderation and, above all, an intuitive and wide-ranging knowledge of yourself.

12
Getting Good
Improvement often comes quickly;
unfortunately, so does stagnation

A BEGINNING RIDER of my acquaintance has become increasingly fascinated with the process of his development. He is awed by what he is now able to do, things which several months ago were unthinkable. He has a naive faith in his infinite progress and is convinced that if the present rate continues he will be a Senior I, a 54-minute time trialist and a national champion before two years are out.

Unfortunately, it doesn't work that way. For any rapidly improving beginner to avoid frustration and disappointment, three different but related facts concerning the development of fitness must be recognized:

1. The curve of improvement will flatten out markedly as you approach the upper limits of your potential.

2. Those upper limits are tipped off by clear physiological signals.

3. Workouts have to be altered in both intensity and duration as you become more fit.

The initial development of fitness follows two rules. First, it is uneven. There is often a series of rapid improvements followed by plateaus in which little progress is made. These periods of stagnation can be frustrating for the rider and the temptation is to increase the workload in an attempt to jolt the body out of its apparent slump. It is better to continue moderate and carefully planned training, secure in the knowledge that the next breakthrough is near. Trying to accelerate the process will only lead to failure of the adaptive process, resulting in a longer plateau or a descent into chronic fatigue caused by overtraining. The physiological changes upon which better performances depend take time to develop; new capillaries and more efficient enzyme systems don't grow overnight. More work is not a panacea. Patience is as great a virtue as perspiration.

The second rule affecting the development of fitness states that the closer you come to your genetic potential, the more time and effort will be required for small gains. When you first begin to ride you will improve rapidly, increasing both speed and distance with breath-taking ease. This dramatic progress often causes new cyclists to become so excited that they project their improvements as if on a graph: "If I continue my present program, I'll be riding 57 minutes for the 25-mile TT by next year." (Fill in your favorite fantasy.) But there's the rub. That rapid rate of improvement won't continue. It might take only two months of steady work to reduce your first time trial attempt of 1:03 to one hour even, but the next three-minute improvement will come harder and take much longer.

The decreasing rate of improvement is comparable to the mathematical and logical paradox which states that you can never get to a given point if you can cover only half the remaining distance on each attempt. If the imaginary point is your physical maximum and you are 10 minutes away, the first jump will be five minutes for a given volume of work and time. But with the same amount of training the next improvement will be only half that big, the next will be half of that, and soon enormous amounts of time and effort will have to be invested for miniscule gains.

If 150 carefully structured miles a week makes you a one-hour time trialist, increasing the mileage to 300 may produce an additional improvement measured only in seconds. Or it may strain you so much, given available rest time and your body's ability to recover, that you will get worse instead of better. It is a sort of physiological law of diminishing return. You have to decide if the additional eight hours a week in training time, the chances of overstress and breakdown, and the increased psychic energy you'll need to pour into your effort are worth a 30- or 40-second gain in performance. For an upwardly mobile Senior I competitor it may be the margin between success and failure on the national level. For the casual rider who has more modest goals as well as interests and responsibilities outside cycling, it may be merely wasted time.

When potential is approached

A number of clear physiological signals will indicate that you are approaching your potential. The most obvious is a steady decline in the rate of improvement. You will recognize this if you keep an accurate record of your performances. Race placings are useful but not very objective, given the variation in courses and

What does it take to make it to the top in international cycling like Andy Hampsten and Greg LeMond? Many miles of hard training, of course. But don't let dreams of winning the Tour de France lead you into trying to do too much too soon. Fitness comes in stages and you must carefully monitor your body's signals if you want to continue improving and yet avoid the dangers of overtraining.

strategy. TT times are better and provide a more valid comparison of fitness from month to month as well as over your whole career.

Another signal is the behavior of the heart rate. As you develop initial fitness the resting pulse will gradually slow because your heart is becoming more efficient. The rate of the slowing will decrease until similar readings are obtained over a period of several months. I have commented earlier that I find daily fluctuations in heart rate to be an unreliable method of gauging short-term recovery from training stress. But a bottoming out of the resting rate over a relatively long time period is a reliable indication that you are at or near maximum form.

A decline in the percentage of body fat to minimum levels is another good tip-off. Although this is conducive to good cycling performance, it is not necessarily good for general health and strength if the process is carried too far. Fat represents stored energy reserves and when these are depleted the body will react by shutting down all but its basic functions. The adaptive system will cease to operate and improvement will slow or stop. Yet athletes the world over strive — often artificially through reduced caloric intake — for very low levels of body fat and then subject themselves to the intense stress of training and competition.

A male gets no vivid warnings when his body fat reaches a precariously low level. Therefore, he has to become aware of his optimum amount by undergoing careful laboratory measurements or by subjectively monitoring his reserves during hard training and long races. Women, on the other hand, may receive more obvious signals. According to some recent research, lowered fat reserves can apparently cause some female endurance athletes to cease menstruating. This has been observed in distance runners, swimmers and gymnasts and is becoming more common as women take up endurance sports more seriously and in greater numbers. The theory is that the body realizes when fat levels have declined too low to support a pregnancy so it shuts down the reproductive capacity. In any case, low and stable body fat levels indicate that your room for improvement is getting smaller.

How to alter training

How should workouts be altered when you near your physical potential and begin to experience slowed improvement? What changes can you introduce into your training that will help you get the maximum benefit out of the time you choose to devote to cycling?

The beginning rider usually trains moderately in a daily program of steady distance for aerobic conditioning. Such a routine is important to help a newcomer develop a cardiovascular base or allow an experienced rider to regain form during the pre-season.

However, when you begin to reach good form you need to alter the pattern. The type and intensity of training needed for the fit rider is quantitatively and qualitatively different than for the novice. We're dealing here with engines in different stages of development.

For example, few people stop to realize that the slowed improvement which accompanies gains in fitness actually means that, as a fit athlete, you are not the same person you were when you first began cycling. The racer who happily proclaims that he feels like a new person since he began regular training is not speaking idly. The acquisition of fitness stimulates profound changes in the physical body as well as the mental outlook.

On a simple level consider the problem of stressing the body enough to create improvement. As a beginner you can do it by riding perhaps 20 miles at 18 m.p.h. This will get your heart rate up near your anaerobic threshold and stimulate all sorts of improvement even though you are not going very fast compared to what you'll later be capable of. In six months you will be so much better that the same ride will not help at all. It will be much too easy for your new fitness level. You may need 40 miles at 21 m.p.h. to stress your vastly improved cardiovascular system. Obviously, if you continue to train with the same degree of output you will remain mired at the same performance level.

Although it may seem like a paradox, there is another adjustment you may need to make in addition to increasing workout intensity. You may need more easy/rest days.

As a new rider you can't go hard enough to get down into your reserves. You get tired after 20 or 30 miles, you breathe hard, your legs ache, but you have plenty of strength and extra energy in the form of stored body fat. You just aren't fit enough to do much damage to deep reserves or drive yourself past your usual and superficial quitting points.

You can, of course, get hurt by overworking and going beyond your limits. If you have never ridden farther than 40 miles and you get into a fast 60-mile training ride with better riders, you will get exhausted. However, your leg muscles will cramp or you will develop knee problems before you reach into the basic strength that is saved only for emergencies. The new rider is not physically capable of touching this reserve except under conditions of extreme emergency and psychic shock, which the usual race situation, emotion charged as it may be, does not produce.

On the other hand, the fit rider is stronger and more capable of going really hard and long, placing enormous stresses on the body.

But as we have seen, the more fit you are the closer you are to overtraining and breakdown. As Dr. George Sheehan has observed, the athlete at the peak of form is only one small step from disaster.

Consider yourself as a fit cyclist who goes out for a 40-miler after work, gets inspired, and rides very hard. You do jams, sprints and hard hills. Because of your excellent fitness you go much faster and much closer to your limits than you could when you were still developing form. Emotionally you are so stoked by your improvement and race success that all training rides are done in a state of terminal excitement. You push and push some more. However, you pay a price. You can't do this too often or you will not be able to recover. A bike racer doesn't live by enthusiasm alone.

Here is where you can get into real trouble. You are no longer playing around with sore legs or strained ligaments; you are stressing the body on levels it saves for survival situations. This may sound overly dramatic, but it isn't. The body has a finite capacity to improve and be healthy; the mind has an infinite capacity to dream of higher goals and order the body to reach them. At some point the mind's goals and the adaptive ability of the body will diverge.

For all these reasons it is important to try to know exactly where your fitness is at any given time in relation to your potential. This can be done only by carefully monitoring the symptoms and signs of fitness: percent of body fat, performance, heart rate and your general feelings of vigor or exhaustion.

13
Time Budgeting
*Planning and desire are needed
to fit daily training into a busy life*

IT IS 6 A.M. Outside his home in Boulder, Colorado, bike racer Mike Nettles pedals off into the cold and gloom on his way to IBM where he is an engineer. He has been up since 5, eaten, and packed his handlebar bag with the clothes he will need for the day. Now he is beginning a 20-mile trip that will include a warm-up, fast spinning in low gears and some interval training. He will be dressed and at his desk by 7:15. After work he will ride another 20-50 miles. In addition to his demanding professional responsibilities, Mike is married and the father of two daughters.

Like other dedicated racers who must prepare to meet strong competition in spite of inadequate time to train, Nettles knows it is still possible to perform well. His example shows that full-time work, family commitments and the desire to race can be efficiently interwoven in one's life. But it goes even further than that because a limited-time competitor must also fit in the rest that is necessary for maximum adaptation. Scheduling everything into a 24-hour period requires maximum use of time-budgeting techniques.

Commuting for fitness

The first step is to commute by bike. In this way the time normally spent sitting in a car is used productively as part of the training day, and you won't have to steal so many minutes from other responsibilities. A 10-mile ride to work or school will take about 30 minutes. Even if you do nothing else for training, that is still a round trip of 20 miles of cycling each weekday, a fairly substantial amount. Of course, the trip home can be lengthened as much as time, daylight and energy will allow. But the important thing is that a decent workout can be squeezed into a time slot that was formerly wasted. You have created training time where none existed before; you have lengthened the day by an hour or so.

This plan works. In 1985 Wayne Stetina was National Road

Champion on 150 miles per week, most of it from commuting rides to his job at Shimano.

At the other end of the commuting spectrum is Jeff Parsons, who lives in Boulder and was a student at the University of Northern Colorado in Greeley, 60 miles away. He frequently commuted to class at an LSD pace, did no speed work, and yet won a Colorado Road Championship.

In addition to the obvious benefits of commuting by bike, there are some not so visible. One is that you'll arrive at the job refreshed and alert. It may be tough to get up earlier, but the physical and mental lift of exercise will carry you through that 10 a.m. let-down that your sedentary colleagues experience. Instead of coffee and junk food at the midmorning break, you can have some fruit or yogurt which will fuel you right on through to lunch.

A bigger reward, though, comes when the whistle blows. Everyone else is feeling groggy, irritable and lethargic from the hassles of the day, and they still have to face a boring drive home. But you can ride, clearing cobwebs and blowing away job-related frustrations. This will help you arrive home relaxed, refreshed and ready for evening responsibilities or a constructive family experience.

Training to and from work can even help you professionally. The aforementioned Mike Nettles says that his daily commuting ride makes him more visible in a large company. It provides him with an instant identity in an organization where anonymity is the rule rather than the exception. Of course, what you do with this visibility depends upon your ability on the job. But it may be just the edge needed for a more successful career.

Overcoming the disadvantages

Cycling to work has some built-in disadvantages but they are not insurmountable. Clothes, lunch, papers and other accouterments of your job can be carried in a small backpack. Get a teardrop-shaped model like those sold at bike and mountaineering shops. You don't need the expensive type with the leather bottom; this will only add weight. Be sure it has a good waist strap to eliminate swaying and bouncing as you ride. The teardrop shape will fit the contour of your back and you'll be surprised at how soon you forget the pack is even there.

I suggest keeping a pair or two of shoes at work so you don't have their weight and sharp edges in the pack. Thanks to the modern permanent press fabrics for pants, shirts and ties, you can roll your clothes neatly and they'll be free of wrinkles when you arrive. Another method is to take the week's clothes to work on Monday morning and shuttle them home Friday afternoon, or whatever logistical arrangement fits your situation. Experiment to find what works best.

Everyone has a fear of smelling like a gorilla's armpit at work all day but such social misgivings are unfounded. Dr. George Sheehan contends that athletic sweat has no odor and he merely towels off after his run. For the more fastidious, I have found that a quick once-over with a washcloth soaked in rubbing alcohol is as good as a shower. It is wise to at least clean the crotch area to help prevent the buildup of skin bacteria which can lead to saddle sores.

Dressing facilities should pose no problem if you are alert to the possibilities. If you are lucky you may have access to a large washroom. Storage rooms are another good choice; ask the person in charge to get you a key so you can lock it while you change. I could use the locker room at the high school where I teach, but I save time by changing in my classroom. I carry the bike in at 7:50, lock the door, and 10 minutes later emerge dressed and ready for student conferences or meetings.

Another alternative is to find a friendly gas station owner near your place of business who will let you use his restroom. Except in unusual circumstances there will always be someplace where you can convert from super racer to mild-mannered businessman, although I would not recommend a phone booth.

Workday training

Here are some specific schemes for piling on the miles in a restricted time framework.

Cycle to work in the morning with clothes and lunch in the pack. A ride of 5-10 miles is adequate. Don't go hard; the purpose is to loosen up and get some steady aerobic miles. Also, you are more susceptible to injury if you go hard when the body is cold and stiff, as it is early in the day.

Thanks to the smooth nature of pedaling you can have breakfast before leaving. I find that a cooked cereal like oatmeal or a combination of grains digests easier and faster than cold cereals. However, a friend of mine does intervals on the way to work one hour after eating granola, fruit and whole wheat toast smeared with peanut butter. He must have a case-hardened digestive tract. Experiment with breakfast, but be sure to eat a good one sometime during the morning. I have even carried breakfast with me and eaten whole grain bread, bananas and other fruit between morning classes.

After work, incorporate a regular training session into the trip home. Scout out a longer route and ride for an hour or more as time and commitments allow. I ride the five miles home, hang the pack on my mailbox as I spin past, and head off to one of my favorite courses. You'll find that you can incorporate a wide variety of training schemes into an after-work session. Intervals, time trials, even LSD are all possible.

The great advantage of this system is that it saves time. You'll be back home to have dinner with the family because the time normally spent driving to and from work has been used as part of your training. Using this system it is possible to get in a substantial number of quality miles during the week and then use the weekend for longer rides or racing.

Early bird special

Not everyone has an 8-to-5 job, of course, but there are plenty of ways to get in the daily workout regardless of your schedule. If you can't train in the afternoon, consider an early morning workout. Where I live it is light enough to ride at 5:45 a.m. by the middle of March, and a month later I can be on the road at 5. It's best not to train in the dark, but with a good light and reflectors on the bike you can be relatively safe. At dawn there are few cars on the road and it is getting lighter every minute.

Early morning workouts have some drawbacks, none of which are insurmountable. Getting up in the pre-dawn hours creates enormous psychological survival problems for certain people. This may be the ultimate test of whether you really want to be a bicycle racer. You will have to give up preconceived notions of your inability to function before noon. Roll out of bed the minute the alarm rings and don't think about anything. He who hesitates is lost. The longer you lie there thinking about how early it is, the harder it becomes to extricate yourself from between the sheets. The first several weeks are the hardest; it then becomes routine as the body and mind accustom themselves to the new schedule.

The other main disadvantage to getting up early is the danger of sleep loss. You will need to make up the deficit with an earlier bedtime, and this can be hard to do. But it is vital to get enough rest since lack of sleep can lead to deep fatigue and overtraining. Time, like matter, can be neither created nor destroyed, so time budgeting is merely a matter of borrowing from one activity and transferring it to another. The early workout steals from sleep and this deficit must be repaid.

After several years of pedominantly early morning training, I find I prefer it. There is little traffic, the wind and heat are usually not problems, and morning is the most beautiful time of day in southwestern Colorado. In addition, the feeling of accomplishment that I get from my riding is a positive way to start the day; that success carries over into other activities.

Perhaps the biggest advantage of sunrise cycling is that workouts are seldom interrupted. That time is your own. Afternoons, however, have a way of getting filled up with the unexpected. If I get my workout in early I can then handle whatever the day throws at me; if I put it off until later I have a fixed anxiety that it will get bumped by other responsibilities, an anxiety that can only be appreciated by the serious athlete.

Midnight rider

Some people, psychologists tell us, are more effective during the late evening and at night. Their mechanisms don't seem to function until after lunch and they may as well not be awake for all the efficiency they generate during the morning hours. If you fit this category, or if your schedule prohibits riding until your workday is done, the late training session might work well.

Try riding from 10 p.m. to midnight. The advantages are considerable. If you have normal job hours, 10 to 12 is almost always open. Even some evening meetings are no obstacle. On the home front, the kids are in bed, the chores around the house complete, and the sedentary night owl is probably reading or watching TV. Workouts at these hours represent good use of time.

Also, the evening workout fits well into the usual meal schedule. A moderate dinner at 6 or 7 p.m. will allow the stomach to be empty by workout time. As an additional benefit this provides motivation not to overeat.

Late evening can be a pleasant time to train. In the summer the air will be cooler, while in colder months evenings aren't as nippy as early mornings. Fewer cars mean less pollution and auto interference. Some cyclists say they concentrate better when they can't see distracting sights along the way. Mentally, the late workout can be a kind of reward after the stresses of the day.

Finally, some cyclists like to separate their sport from their professional and family lives as much as possible. The late workout not only removes training from the usual family and job

The late Bob Cook, one of America's finest climbers, is shown completing a lap of the merciless Morgul-Bismarck course during the 1980 Coors Classic. Just 23 years old when claimed by cancer, he set a record that may never be broken when he powered to six victories in six starts in the 28-mile Mt. Evans Hill Climb. The race has been renamed in his memory. Among Cook's many accomplishments was finding the time to ride an average of 10,000 miles a year while forging a 3.9 grade average in engineering at the University of Arizona. His combination of talent and dedication earned him a place on the National Road Team in 1977-80 and he was a 1980 Olympian.

hours, it also provides a degree of anonymity to the training — under the cover of darkness as it were.

However, the big drawback is that same darkness. Riding at night is dangerous because you can't see road hazards very well and motorists can't see you. Carting around lighting systems doesn't have much appeal, so many night trainers like to use lighted parks or suburban streets. This may require a loop course which can be boring but will work.

Some cyclists simply prefer night riding. Steve Dayton, for example, has trained at night on Indianapolis streets riding a bike equipped with clinchers, generator lights, reflectors — the works. He maintains that the added weight helps increase his strength without destroying suppleness, and it is his experience that he is actually safer at night since traffic is lighter than during the day.

Overtraining can be just as much a concern with the late workout as the early one if the schedule means you lose time in bed. The problem will be compounded if you are one of those athletes who gets charged up by workouts and has trouble falling asleep afterward. Personally, I'd rather use that energy positively as a springboard for my day rather than have it interfere with my rest.

Another disadvantage is a lack of carryover to races. Some athletes report that they get so used to training in the dark they experience a sense of disorientation when they compete in daylight. A more serious problem is the disruption of bodily cycles. Most races are early morning affairs and it is hard for the human body, creatures of habit that we are, to make the abrupt transition and still operate at peak efficiency. The principle of specificity which should guide the overall scheme of workouts means that training sessions should resemble the actual conditions under which races will be run.

All in all, the late workout is certainly feasible and is employed by a number of athletes either by choice or necessity. But unless your preferences run that way it can be incredibly hard on enthusiasm and morale.

Four-day work week

With the advent of the four-day work week, some riders are finding that they can get in very few miles on their 10-hour workdays but otherwise have excess time. This situation is not as bad as it first appears. In fact, it has a positive aspect: It enables the racer to go long and/or hard on three consecutive days, resulting in heavy stresses to the adaptive mechanism. Light/ short days the remainder of the week give the body time to recuperate and to consolidate the gains made during the tough workouts.

Of course, three days hard followed by four days of job stress, little sleep, overeating and general sloth may produce more harm than benefit. Such a schedule could turn the serious racer into a weekend athlete and convert healthy training into heart attack country. Dr. Ken Cooper says it best: "I know when the weekend athlete will die — on a weekend." However, the principle of hard/ easy can apply here if those four days are used for short and light exercise to keep the muscles loose.

For example, the ambitious cyclist with three days off each week could ride 80-100 miles of LSD on Friday, 40 miles with intervals on Saturday, and 60-70 miles of random jams, time trials and motorpacing on Sunday. He could then take Monday as a rest day and squeeze in 20 miles of easy spinning on Tuesday, Wednesday and Thursday. These shorter rides could be done as commuting. Such a schedule provides for about 250 miles a week, including three hard days and optimum recovery time. Weekend races are effective substitutes for the stressful training. If the race is short, get in more miles afterward to fill in the schedule and build toward long-term goals.

It is important to work gradually into this type of program because the strain of three consecutive hard workouts could lead to injury. The advantage is that intense stress induced in this way will stimulate a profound adaptation, building reserves and strength.

The combined schedule

When looking at the number of hours needed for training each week, it is obvious that very few cyclists will have their responsibilities in life so rigidly scheduled that they can always be sure of a certain time slot for their riding. Employers and teachers can demand all sorts of odd-hour duties, and families are notorious for causing changes to private plans at the last moment. If you are as compulsively ordered as I am, such disruptions can be tremendously frustrating. However, like most apparent disasters, these can be turned to advantage if you apply a little creativity.

In the area of training schedules, the solution is a plan that combines a variety of early morning, afternoon and evening workouts as well as a double session once in a while. Let's look at a week in March from my training diary and see how such a plan actually worked. An early season road race was three weeks away, so it was crucial that I continued to get in long miles. However, I also needed to do some intervals for the general seasonal buildup and upcoming criteriums. Ordinarily this would pose no particular problem. But my work schedule was tight in the worst possible places, necessitating odd-hour workouts that would cut into time for recovery. The week looked like a real challenge in terms of balancing stress and rest.

MONDAY: Ah, Monday — especially coming off a tough 65-mile ride with jams and some motorpacing on Sunday. I needed to ride about 25 easy miles to stretch and loosen the legs so that this week's work would be of high quality. But I had to be at school at 8 a.m. to confer with some students, I had five classes to teach and I had to moderate a film forum from 7 to 10 p.m. In addition, my wife's running workout was from 5 to 5:45 p.m. and I had to look after our young son. So I had two alternatives, the first of which was to get up at 5, ride 20 miles from 5:45 to 6:45, shower, eat and pedal five miles into school and then home afterwards. I weighed the advantages: The weather would be cold in the morning but I would miss the afternoon's precipitation if the weather pattern of the last few days held. On the other hand, if I got up early I would lose more than an hour of sleep that I needed to help my recuperation after Sunday. The other choice was to sleep in until 6:30, pedal to school and ride afterward from 3:30 to 5. I would get my rest, but it meant taking a chance on unforeseen disruptions, not to mention hail, sleet and gloom of night.

I opted for the extra sleep, figuring that I'd better not start the week tired. As it turned out, it snowed on me during the last half of the ride but let up before my wife's run. While she was out I played with Ross, cleaned the bike, showered and put the finishing touches on dinner so we could eat in time to get me to the film forum. One day down.

TUESDAY: I needed a big day but rest was going to be a problem — my regular classes were surrounded by one meeting at 8 a.m. and another from 8 to 10 p.m. However, when you need miles you need miles. So I decided to take a chance. Up at 5, I rode from 5:15 to 7 and did intervals and three hill jams during the 35 miles. I showered, ate and made it to the early meeting. Every second counts — I ate oatmeal intead of granola for breakfast because it doesn't take as long to chew. Only the experienced limited-time racer would appreciate that, or the fear of a flat tire which would destroy the whole schedule.

I felt a little drained during the day but got out for another 30 miles after teaching. During the evening meeting I was feeling the effects and went over in my mind the advice I am always getting and giving about sufficient rest.

WEDNESDAY: No meetings on the schedule. The weather was clearing so I enjoyed the luxury of sleeping until 6:30 and then commuted easily into school. I felt good in the morning but the day turned hectic: student conferences while gulping lunch, five classes spent wrestling with Yeats' poetry, and a parent conference after school that I didn't find out about until noon. By 2 p.m. I was sleepy, irritable and exhausted. After the conference I pedaled slowly home, scrapping plans for a brisk 20 miles. In the evening I tried to grade papers but gave up the heroic struggle and went to bed at 9.

THURSDAY: I woke up at 6:30, feeling better. I did not set the alarm, allowing my body the chance to wake me at 5 if it did not need the sleep. But it did. I rode into work briskly. After school I felt energized and did 30 miles, including a five-mile time trial at close to my personal record for the course. My exercise high lasted through the three-hour evening class I teach at a local college.

FRIDAY: I woke at 5 to wind and an inch of icy snow on the roads. I wanted to ride at a moderate pace early in the day so I would have nearly 24 hours to recover before my long weekend ride. Instead I looked out the window and crawled back in the sack. My wife muttered something about showing a little sense for once. She should talk; she will run in the dark in a blizzard. Later I put riding clothes in the car and drove to work, changed after school, drove home and rode 25 miles on the cleared roads. The weather was improving so in the evening I prepared for my long ride.

SATURDAY: I like to schedule my long ride for Saturday so that if I am unable to go I still have Sunday. For the same reason I prefer to go early, even though I usually have all day to fit it in. In this way I also escape most of the wind that is an inevitable feature of spring in Colorado.

I got up at 6 and ate a small bowl of oatmeal and a banana, stuffed an apple and some dates into my jersey pocket, and was riding by 7. It was 25 F degrees when I left but I would rather have it cool than windy. I did 65 miles on a hilly course, with emphasis on high cadence and a supple style. I jammed the hills hard and included a five-mile time trial simulation about halfway out when the spirit moved me. Twenty miles from home a farm truck full of hay lumbered past. I sprinted to get on and motorpaced the incredulous rancher until he turned off on a gravel road.

SUNDAY: I spun out an easy 15 miles late in the day after a family cross-country ski trip and picnic to the nearby mountains.

What was accomplished for the week? A total of 260 miles. One long, continuous ride of 65 miles and a 70-mile day based on a split workout. Two short time trials. One interval session. Other jams and fartlek-type increases in intensity scattered throughout the week.

Also fatigue. A 260-mile week is not overpowering, but I had little time to recover from the training. The stress of the workouts was intensified by the stress of my teaching, my daily routine and restricted sleep. I have found that I can handle this sort of schedule on alternate weeks for several early season months if I have built solid reserves over the winter. However, I must ease off by June or I will fall victim to deep fatigue caused not so much by overtraining as by underresting. I find that I then have to pay careful attention to what my body is telling me. This is where training diverges from science and becomes equal parts of intuition, luck and art.

Successful training in a limited-time framework is not an easy task. Consistently fitting a quality workout into a tight schedule requires numerous adjustments to the normal routine. I think that the sacrifices which the mature racer must make help explain why he is often more successful than younger riders who have more time.

If you want to race badly enough to create time for training, you will probably make sure your workouts are of high quality. On the other hand, if to you this all seems too much trouble, perhaps you should examine your motives and the intensity of your desire to compete before berating yourself for lack of an iron will. If it isn't enjoyable, don't do it.

14
LSD

*Long steady distance is no cure-all
but the proper dose will surely help*

LONG STEADY DISTANCE as a training philosophy has
achieved almost the status of a religion. It is the technique of
covering many miles at an even aerobic pace and to some degree it
has always been a feature of cycling tours as well as running for
fitness. In times past, such steady efforts enabled soldiers and
messengers to cover prodigious distances. More recently, revered
running coaches such as Percy Cerutty and Arthur Lydiard have
made endurance the cornerstone of their training programs.

But endurance-based workouts had no name and no press agent
until Joe Henderson, at the time an editor at *Runner's World*
magazine, coined the phrase "long slow distance." This coincided
exactly with the running boom of the 1970s and its popularity was
immediate and nearly overpowering. The slow pace appealed to
former competitive trackmen who were burned out on intervals. It
appealed to the overweight beginning runner because slow was the
only choice he had. Additionally, the initials LSD by which the
technique has become known glance rather obviously at the drug
culture while emphasizing the much publicized addictive nature of
endurance sports. Lately the "slow" has been replaced by
"steady" to give a more accurate concept of what the training
regimen calls for.

As an offshoot to running, LSD training for cycling has been
hailed as a cure-all for every conceivable malady from a lack of
endurance to a faulty pedal stroke. It's not, of course, but it does
have some important benefits.

Runners claim that they can go long and slow in training, then
manage a race pace more than a minute per mile faster. In cycling,
LSD has fostered a massive-miles syndrome where distance is
accumulated not only for the indisputable benefits it produces but
also for a kind of mystical experience that, it is implied, makes the
rider better by a kind of physiological osmosis. The results,
advocates say, are far greater than the bare bones of the training

The middle letter in LSD should stand for steady, not slow. Keep your cadence and heart rate high and don't let the ride turn into a sightseeing excursion. On the other hand, it's best not to cross the anaerobic threshold during this type of training. Try to work at a level which fosters the optimum training effect for you, as determined by the heart rate formula in this chapter.

method would seem to promise. There are riders who do only LSD rides in training, never going faster except in actual races.

The dangers of worshipping LSD to the exclusion of other training methods such as intervals and time trials are obvious. The principle of specificity of exercise states that you get what you train for. A steady diet of LSD prepares you for long, evenly paced rides, not the varying pace, frequent accelerations and brutal jams of racing. However, LSD has some definite advantages and it should be included, with discretion, in your training program. In general, LSD provides aerobic stress that builds long-term strength, rather than tearing down the body as can speed work.

In the steady effort of the classic LSD ride no lactic acid is produced. It is theorized that this substance, a by-product of hard (anaerobic) exercise, can build up in the system. The resulting tendency of the blood pH to become acidic can create all sorts of unpleasant side effects, from persistent fatigue to depression. Regardless of whether there is a solid physiological base for this assertion, it is certain that the lower intensity of LSD training is easier to sustain mentally over years of training.

Secondly, an extended period of LSD riding will build a solid endurance base. It will transform you into a cyclist capable of sustained effort. You will develop a big and powerful heart, an efficient blood transportation system and favorable enzyme activity in the cells. Without such a base, any speed work you attempt will be counterproductive.

LSD also burns fat. At heart rates of around 150, fat is an important fuel in the energy producing process. As a result your body becomes trained to go longer before bonking from glycogen depletion, and excess fat is gradually used up. This produces a lean, efficient cyclist. Finally, LSD mentally accustoms you to spending hours at a time on the bike. A hundred miles becomes routine rather than an overpowering burden.

How long? How slow?

On the surface nothing could be simpler than an LSD workout. Just go out and ride for a few hours, right? Well, like most training techniques it isn't quite that easy.

How long is long? The rule of thumb is to make the mileage as long as your longest race, but some riders modify this to read as much time in the saddle as the longest race. Hence, a Senior III or IV would ride either 50-75 miles or about three hours on LSD days. Be aware that there is a lower limit to length if a ride is to do any physiological good. The purpose of the long ride is to burn some fat and to develop the aerobic system. The way I read the current research, an LSD session that lasts less than two hours isn't of much value after you have become reasonably fit.

How slow is slow? Not as slow as some riders think. You mustn't let LSD rides degenerate into sightseeing tours with your heart rate hovering around 120. For most riders this will be below the intensity at which the training effect takes place.

To determine the heart rate level which will stimulate improvement in your own body, first estimate your maximum heart rate by subtracting your age in years from 220. Then subtract your resting heart rate from your maximum rate and take 75% of the resulting number (in other words, multiply by 0.75). Add the answer back to the resting rate and you have the number of beats per minute at which your heart must work to ensure physiological benefits. For example, a 30-year-old rider has a theoretical maximum heart rate of 190 (220 minus 30) and he finds his resting pulse to be 60. Subtracting 60 from 190 gives 130, and 75% of that is about 98. Adding 98 and 60 gives 158, the approximate pulse rate this rider should maintain during LSD rides if he is to get near-maximum improvement for his time on the bike.

This is not an easy level of exertion. In fact, it is real work when extended to three or four hours. However, I suspect that if you spin out your weekly LSD ride at a more comfortable pace you are fooling yourself about its benefits. It is difficult enough for a heavily committed cyclist to find time for a long ride without wasting the hours in the saddle. I recommend that you make every effort to keep your exertion level high enough to produce your optimum heart rate. Most riders will find that maintaining a 90-95 cadence in a gear around 70 inches, say 42x17 or 16, will do the trick and also help cultivate a smooth spin.

On the other hand, discipline is required to keep from going too hard. A long ride on the plateau of the training effect can be boring in its demand for a steady level of discomfort. You need to concentrate on your energy output so that the heart rate stays steady, but you aren't working hard enough to fully engage the mind. It just grinds away at you. The temptation is to either slow down or sprint up a hill or against a farm truck for a little variety. Be careful. Such bursts of speed produce lactic acid, which is exactly what you don't want in this sort of training.

Laying the base

The pre-season is the most important time to do long workouts because it is then that the base is laid for the season's racing. Unfortunately, this is also when the weather is worst in most sections of the country. While a 25-mile ride with intervals can be done in miserable conditions (you are suffering anyway, so what is a little sleet?), 100 miles in a February snowstorm is something else again.

One way to avoid the problem is to combine training methods in the pre-season. For example, if you need an LSD workout but the weather is abysmal, begin with whatever length ride is tolerable — say one hour. When you return, change into dry clothes and go running for another hour. Then finish up with 30 minutes on the rollers. The cardiovascular system will be stressed over a long period of time but you will avoid frostbite and other perils of winter.

I suppose you could substitute a long run of about 20 miles for an LSD workout on the bike. But, once again harping back to the principle of specificity, running can't adequately substitute for cycling, given the biomechanical differences in the two activities. The unaccustomed pounding of a two-hour run could also produce ligament and joint problems in a cyclist who hasn't been incorporating running into his program for a number of weeks. I confess that I like long runs but can rarely do them; my knee invariably protests regardless of the number of stars my shoes boast or the cleverly engineered orthotic devices I glue to the insoles to correct my various sins of posture and alignment. I keep trying, but when cycling is impossible a better LSD choice is a long cross-country ski tour.

Scheduling the workout

The major problem with LSD training in any season is finding the time to do it. By definition LSD takes time — three hours at least. That limits most riders to the weekend. Here is where planning and self-discipline are important. A short midweek interval session can always be rescheduled for the next day, but a long ride penciled in for Sunday and postponed will have to wait at least six days before a suitable chunk of time is again available.

One way out of this problem is to use split workouts. It is possible to ride 40 miles between 5:30 and 7:30 a.m. and another 30 miles after work, but such a schedule is physically and mentally tough. It may also not produce as much fitness as a continuous ride of the same total distance. It can work, however, as John Allis showed by using split sessions in his training for the Olympics. He was employed full-time and he rode 40 miles before work and another 40 in the evening. But he cautions that such a schedule cannot be maintained for long and it requires a solid base of reserve strength.

I find that split workouts are feasible if they are done no more than once a week. Two rides daily seem more wearing than one of equal length because the training stress is compounded by job stress and extra time is needed to get ready twice and cleaned up twice. If you do try the split LSD routine, increase the distance of each segment slowly and be sure to get enough rest to make up for the sleep lost in the early morning.

What can you do if it's just impossible to fit in the one long ride per week that experts insist is minimum preparation for road racing? One solution is to ride long races anyway and take your chances. As mentioned last chapter, Wayne Stetina was able to win the 1985 National Road Championship in 1976 on around 150 miles a week. He did it through a combination of talent, skill, smart riding and, I suspect, an impressive capacity for suffering. Jim Montgomery, multi-National Champion Veteran rider, rarely trains over an hour at a time but regularly wins major road races. Some people seem to possess what can be called natural endurance.

However, almost everyone who can't train long would do best to stay away from the 100-milers and specialize in time trials, shorter road races and criteriums. Most riders demonstrate that inexorable training maxim that you get what you work for. If you try to race 100 miles when your training is only adequate for 50, you get cramps, you get tired, you get the bonk and sooner or later you get dropped.

LSD training is an important component of total race preparation, but if you can't find the time for it you shouldn't be doomed in competition. Simply adjust your goals and expectations to the shorter events to best utilize the amount and type of training that you can do. As we'll see in the next chapter, it is possible to develop plenty of speed and strength in short workouts.

15
Intervals
Embrace them, don't fear them, and come closer to your potential

INTERVALS FRIGHTEN even top-level racers and it's no wonder — this form of training has a reputation for brutality that promises to destroy both body and soul unless done exactly right. As a result, beginners usually find more than enough reasons to avoid them.

Some riders dodge intervals because they did them in other sports and are not anxious to repeat the experience. Ex-swimmers remember the fatigue of repeat 100s, and former trackmen mentally revisit the burning lungs and leaden legs of endlessly repeated 440s. Those from team sports recall wind sprints with a visible hatred. A fellow who came into cycling in his late 20s after an intensely competitive college track career asserted: "I am racing bikes for fun. I have had enough hard training sessions."

In addition to these subjective feelings, riders have read or heard stories of physical problems arising from an overdose of intervals. Sportsmedicine authorities talk in hushed tones about such exotic maladies as "energy-dynamic heart insufficiency" as one possible result of a poorly administered interval program. Even if no physical horrors result, erratic performances are associated with intervals in the minds of many riders.

The prospect of mental fatigue is another factor that frightens riders away. The mind is capable of extending just so much effort and enduring just so much pain. Some riders suffer to such an extent during training that they have no psychic energy left for racing. I once asked a retired rider why he quit. "I just got tired of hurting," he replied, citing all the pain he had endured on the bike. Nearly every example was from training rides using intervals.

In the final analysis it is mostly the mystique of intervals that seems to frighten the beginning rider away. Bjarne Rostaing, writing in *Velo-news* about Alan Kingsbery, commented that the rider "sees no point in the hurting of intervals." If a cyclist like Kingsbery, a former Olympic team member, avoided intervals, the novice is likely to reason: What business do I have even considering them?

Yet interval training, properly applied, can be a key to realizing your potential as a racer. Intervals should not be avoided out of ignorance but should instead be done as part of a carefully planned program. Of course, such speed work can be dangerous if used indiscriminately — as they say, speed kills. When done correctly, however, interval training is one of the most important techniques in a bike racer's arsenal.

Interval training is necessary because races don't proceed at an even pace. Energy output in the usual road race or criterium varies widely — from moderate during lulls in the action to gut-wrenching maximum efforts in jams, on hills and in the final sprint. A rider who trains at steady efforts, no matter how close to his anaerobic threshold, will probably not have the speed to continually stay in there when the pace heats up.

Look at it this way: If you can time trial at 25 miles per hour but your top speed in a jam is 29, you could be off the back in the first 10 miles of a race if the pace increases to 32 m.p.h. for a short distance in response to a break. The same is true of the sprint. You could tow the pack for 20 miles with bull-like strength, yet get passed by everyone in the last 200 meters. Bike racing is essentially unfair because a stronger rider can be dropped by a weaker one who has more snap or short-term speed. Obviously, some speed work is necessary if you are to develop as an all-round rider.

How intervals work

The theory behind interval training is to get the heart rate up to a point where large amounts of oxygen are being used (perhaps 80-90% of your max VO2). This involves a pulse of perhaps 170-190 beats per minute for most riders, although this will vary with age. Then the heart rate is allowed to drop to about 120 before the process is repeated. Compared to steady-state riding, interval training allows an enormous amount of work to be done at intense levels, thanks to the rest period between efforts.

Intervals can be ridden in a number of ways. The high technology method is to go hard for perhaps one minute and then take your pulse. (Find it in the big artery next to your Adam's apple; after a hard exertion the throb is easy to locate.) Immediately after the effort keep one hand on the bars, use the other to take the pulse, and read a watch strapped to your wrist or handlebars. Spin easily in a lower gear during this process — don't stop or

Bike racing is an unfair sport in the sense that a rider with short-term speed can sit in and then beat a more powerful opponent. If you are in the latter category, interval training will help give you the snap to answer back.

freewheel. Count the pulse for six seconds and add a zero to get the one-minute figure. The number should be around 180. (To estimate your maximum attainable heart rate, subtract your age from 220.) When the pulse drops to 120, repeat the hard effort. Continue to drive the heart rate to near maximum levels during the "on" phase of the interval but do not repeat the effort until it calms to 120. You may want to invest in an electronic heart rate monitor. They make this business of keeping track of your ticker a lot easier and more accurate.

Heart rate monitoring is supposed to be the most scientific way to perform intervals and it is said to produce the most rapid gains. It appeals to riders with precise minds and also to those who are insecure about their training program. The consistency gives at least the illusion of certainty to the vagueness of physical improvement.

However, some riders find such an interval method mentally destructive — you stare at a watch and the unyielding numbers tell you when you are supposed to be recovered enough to go again. As a result they prefer a method that may be called random

Group training, much like the team time trial, provides a natural interval session as well as practice in following a wheel and working in a pace line. A hard turn at the front is followed by pulling off and slowing slightly to drop back to the end of the line. As each rider rotates through he has a chance to recover in the draft before making another effort against the wind.

intervals or *fartlek*, a Swedish term meaning "speed play," a training method used by distance runners. Here you go hard during a ride whenever the spirit moves you. Sprint for a road sign, jam on a hill, time trial for a mile, attack to catch a slow-moving vehicle or another rider. This method is more unstructured and eliminates the Prussian army aspects of most interval programs. However, it is easy to let up and not do enough or go hard enough to stimulate improvement. Conversely, some riders will push until they drop as long as that clock isn't making them. An unstructured interval program demands discipline from the rider as well as a clear sense of goals.

Regardless of the interval method you choose, time spent between hard efforts should not be spent coasting. Shift to an easier gear and keep spinning at a brisk cadence. This will help remove lactic acid from the muscles and approximate the race situation.

Adding variety

Although interval training is often associated with sheer drudgery, variety is actually one of its strong points. An almost limitless number of variations on basic intervals can be devised, as the following examples show.

•Alternate large and small gears, doing one interval in 67 inches (42x17) and the next in 93 (52x15). This lets you work on both spin and power.

•Using a short hill, go up hard and come down easy a number of times. On a long uphill pedal a certain number of strokes standing in a large gear and the same number seated in something smaller.

•On a moderately traveled road with a wide shoulder, sprint every time a car approaches from behind. You will get some strange looks and you will rarely beat the car, but if you usually train alone any competition is better than none. As a bonus this will force you to learn to ride in a straight line when making a hard effort.

•Do a ladder of 30 seconds on, one minute off; 45 seconds on, one minute off; one minute on, one off; 1:30 on, one off; and then come back down.

•Predetermine several landmarks — signs, trees, mailboxes, etc. — and sprint or jam for each one during the last 10 miles of a longer ride.

•During motorpaced training have a signal to tell the driver when to gradually accelerate, and then hang on until it's impossible. This can be brutal.

•Ride a loop of 20-40 miles and jam every time you see a specific object — every dog, every bluebird, every farm vehicle, every patch of glass on the road, etc.

•Group rides with everyone taking a strong turn at the front are natural interval sessions.

Precautions

Intervals can be more dangerous to your health than other forms of training because they produce high stress loads. Since most of the training is anaerobic, intervals can actually destroy fitness rather than enhance it unless they are monitored carefully. Be aware of the following cautions before you launch your interval program.

A solid base is vital. You need to develop the cardiovascular system before you employ anaerobic training. In addition, hard intervals can cause all sorts of muscle and ligament troubles if you haven't accumulated enough base miles to condition the legs properly. For this reason a pre-season buildup of 1,000-1,500 miles is recommended. This total should be accrued in a low gear of about 63-67 inches (42x18 or 17) using a cadence of 90-100. The emphasis should be on fast, smooth, supple spinning. Avoid big gears, abrupt pace changes and hard jams.

Increase the training load gradually. It usually takes six to eight weeks for the body to respond most effectively to an anaerobic program, so plan your interval training to end just before the race or series of races you want to peak for. Then ease off or eliminate intervals and go back to aerobic rides. If you will be racing fairly frequently this should provide sufficient stress to keep you at a high level of fitness.

Rest is vital. Intervals are addictive and it is easy to overdose. Everyone has his own tolerance to the stresses of interval training, but one session a week is a good place to start. Don't increase the frequency or the intensity unless you are sure you can handle it. Early in the racing season don't cheat and attempt to get better faster by slipping in extra interval sessions. Remember that a race counts as an interval workout.

Carefully monitor your bodily signs during an interval program. Be aware of how you feel. If you are doing intervals frequently and you are tired and dead in the legs, it is a sure bet that you need more rest rather than more work.

Before any speed session be sure to warm up properly. It is important to take time for some stretching and loosening-up exercises before you get on the bike. Start the ride slowly in low gears and progressively increase the ratio and the cadence until you are perspiring freely. Don't go all out on the first interval but try to establish a level of intensity that you can maintain through to the last one. By then fatigue will have you riding at your maximum, but if you've done it right your cadence and riding style won't be falling to pieces.

Don't overgear. Doing so usually fosters a square, plodding pedal stroke, knee trouble and dead legs instead of the fitness you are looking for. Use gears that allow you to keep cadence at race levels — 90-100 r.p.m.

Don't persist in an interval program if you dread the thought, although a little uneasiness before a workout is normal and probably useful; it serves to get some adrenaline into the system and helps make the workout more intense. Real dread, on the other hand, can cause you to use too much of your store of emotional energy in the workout and be left flat and unwilling to suffer in a race.

Finally, intervals aren't for everyone regardless of potential benefit. If you can race often enough you can get all the benefits of anaerobic work without the drudgery of lonely, hard training efforts. However, for the majority of U.S. riders who can race just once a week or less frequently, interval training plays a vital role in becoming fitter and faster.

16
Weight Training
Use the winter to build strength for more riding power next season

DURING THE WINTER, activities other than cycling are useful because they develop muscles that have been neglected during the long months of training and racing. Sports such as skiing, running, basketball and others are also good for getting your mind off the bike for a while so you can return to heavy training mentally refreshed.

Important as these alternate activities are, if you are a serious rider you have to devote at least part of your winter to the specific task of building a solid cycling base for next season. The aerobic portion can be developed through several weekly sessions of riding, running or cross-country skiing. However, the creation of new strength should not be overlooked, and this is best accomplished through a weight program.

Unfortunately, weight training is often misunderstood by athletes and even coaches. One area of confusion is the type of reward that can be expected. Indeed, weight programs are capable of producing a number of diverse results depending on various factors. Soviet super-heavyweight lifter Vasily Alexyev has developed a huge, 350-pound body that makes him look obese, even though he is reputed to have only 12% body fat. American running legend Frank Shorter has added resistance training to his training schedule in recent years but remains lean and trim. Pole vaulters use weights to develop their upper bodies but are able to make impressive improvements in strength without adding bulk. By using weights I gained 50 pounds in 18 months during my college football career, but a friend lost 30 pounds in a year by lifting and jogging just nine miles a week.

Obviously, weight training alone cannot produce such varied results. Other factors are also at work. Heredity is important; some people have a higher percentage of male hormones which tend to produce bulkier muscles. Women in sports are assured that because of their lower level of this hormone they can lift without getting too big. Male bodybuilders and strength athletes who want to bulk up sometimes take anabolic steroids that are supposed to increase the level of certain hormones and promote muscle mass. Diet is also a factor. I suspect that two people of identical genetic make-up who lifted in similar programs but ate 3,000 and 6,000 calories daily, respectively, would see great differences in the results after a year.

Finally, the program itself is important, though probably to a lesser degree than is usually thought. Multiple sets of low repetitions with heavy weights are said to build size, while high repetitions with light weights are supposed to promote endurance and strength without bulk. Yet athletes report such varied results from their programs that many factors, including some we may not even be aware of, are surely at work.

If you have written off weight training for fear you will get too heavy to race effectively, keep in mind that the process of weight gain is an arduous one that does not happen overnight. You can monitor your body weight and easily make adjustments in your training program or diet if you find you are getting too heavy.

Development of strength

Before beginning weight work it is important to understand how strength is developed and retained. During pre-season riding and into the racing season itself, many cyclists neglect their upper bodies because all their time and energy is devoted to getting in the miles. This is not good because all the hard-won strength from a winter weight program will vanish if muscles aren't periodically exercised. You could be much weaker at the end of the racing season when important competitions occur than you were at the beginning; there could be a deterioration in performance that even the increased miles won't help. So it is important to lift during the season to maintain some of the strength gained during the winter. But how do you find the time and energy?

Fortunately, research indicates that the most difficult phase of strength building is the actual acquisition of that strength. Once a muscle has been strengthened, less exercise is needed to keep it strong. In fact, some experts argue that you can achieve maximum strength with one set of 8-15 slow repetitions done to exhaustion.

An insight into the importance of overall physical strength is offered by former pro rider George Mount, who credited a winter weight program with helping him develop the strength needed to improve his sprint and general endurance. Mount, America's best

Olympic cycling performer of the '70s with his sixth place in the road race at Montreal, commented in an interview that "there's two kinds of strength: strength for racing, and then there is (growl-and-grunt) strength for being able to take it, being able to adapt . . . being able to go into a stage race and grow stronger." Training on the bike can produce the first kind of strength, but you can't develop that sort of race fitness without having a strong "growl-and-grunt" body at the start of road training. You can't make a strong rider out of a weak person. And weight training is the most effective way to become strong.

This is good news for the cyclist. I try to build strength during the off-season with one of the programs (circuit training, power training) described below. Once daily on-the-bike training has begun, three times a week I do one set of bent rows, presses behind the neck, situps and squats when I come in from my ride. This takes less than 10 minutes but is sufficient to maintain strength or slightly improve it. When the off-season rolls around I can go to a more rigorous program without having to start from scratch. More important, the strength I gain each year is kept throughout the cycling season.

Circuit training

One way to employ weights effectively is in a circuit training program. This technique has long been used for general conditioning by football players, swimmers and other athletes. Only recently have cyclists begun circuit training, primarily because of the advocacy of USCF National Men's Coach Director Eddie Borysewicz.

Circuit training consists of a short (usually 15 seconds) exercise bout at each of several stations, followed by a rest period of similar length. A number of different exercises are included and the circuit can be repeated several times. The ideal device for such training is a Universal Gym, Nautilus, or similar multi-station machine which simplifies changing the weight and setting up each exercise. These machines are available at gyms, schools and exercise establishments. However, most time-conscious cyclists find it more convenient to do workouts in their own homes with as little equipment as possible, so I will describe one way to set up a circuit. Remember that the advantage of circuit training is its variety; it is possible to perform three circuit workouts a week all winter and never do the same routine twice.

You will need a barbell set (the standard 110 pounds is adequate), a sturdy bench, a carpet scrap to cushion the weights, and some room in a garage or spare bedroom. With this equipment at the ready, this is how I perform my off-season circuit training:

1. I begin with a good warm-up of jogging, riding rollers or calisthenics until I am breathing and sweating freely. I also do the usual stretching movements. Often my circuit is done after riding, running or cross-country skiing and this aerobic activity serves as the warm-up.

2. I do each of the following exercises for 15 seconds and then rest 15 seconds before going on to the next movement. The sequence is important because the same muscle group won't be stressed in consecutive exercises, and exercises for which the same amount of weight is used are lumped together as much as possible, reducing the amount of time spent changing plates. If you don't know the proper way to do each exercise, consult an illustrated guide such as *The Complete Weight Training Book* by Bill Reynolds. Better yet, get someone with experience to show you. Proper form on weight exercises is almost impossible to put into words but crucial for good results; bad form leads to injuries and stalled progress.

3. The exercise sequence is (A) cleans; (B) bent-knee situps; (C) bent rows, after which I reduce the weight for the next exercises; (D) press behind neck; (E) jumpovers — with the barbell on the shoulders and the feet together, jump back and forth over a low box or other obstacle about six inches high, keeping a good rhythm; (F) bench press, then add more weight to bar; (G) squats, using a chair or bench to limit the depth of the squat to the same knee bend that you get at the top of your pedal stroke.

4. Rest two minutes after completing the circuit.

5. Go through circuit a total of three times.

As for the amount of weight on the bar, make it so that you can keep good form during the entire last circuit. Most people tend to use too much. The purpose is not to lift heavy weights but to develop strength and also stress the cardiovascular system. If done right, a circuit should leave you panting hard. Increase the poundage gradually as strength develops, but don't be in too much of a hurry. Slow, progressive adaptation is the key. After all, you have the whole winter.

Also, start off easily with one trip through the circuit. When you first begin a weight program you will be amazed at the soreness that develops from unfamiliar use of the muscles. Don't rush into it unless you want to walk like Robbie the Robot. It may take awhile before you are able to do more than one or two repetitions of the circuit per workout. Monitor your body.

A form of resistance work that can substitute for squats is ergometer-type riding. A bicycle ergometer equipped with racing pedals, saddle, and dropped bars works best because it can be cranked up to high resistance but most riders don't have one because of the prohibitive cost. However, a suitable substitute can be devised with rollers. The easiest way is to purchase a Racer-Mate, the $80 device that rides on the rear tire and increases rolling resistance with fan wheels that catch the air. Otherwise, you can ride the rollers in a big gear with underinflated clinchers, or fold a towel under the rear drum. Also, some wind-load simulators come with two sets of rotating fans for greater resistance. The important thing is to make those pedals hard to turn.

I sometimes use my ergometer as part of the regular circuit. When the routine calls for squats, I get on the bike instead and do one or two minutes hard. If you routinely increase the time and resistance, impressive gains can be made over the winter.

Program for time trialists

Since I strongly encourage riders to give serious attention to time trialing, and since I like TTs so much myself, I've come up with a specialized off-season strength program that could help you produce dramatic gains in races against the clock. This specialized work can be incorporated into the winter program as follows:

1. Circuit training twice a week, followed by three sets of three minutes on your ergometer or substitute. Work hard to increase resistance to the maximum you can handle, keeping at least a 90 cadence.

2. Once a week do a hard weight training session consisting of 5-10 sets of squats (8-10 reps each) with as much weight as you can handle in good form. This is a power routine and you should try for maximum poundage. Some riders should be able to use 500 pounds or more by spring.

3. Twice a week get on the road for a short, easy aerobic ride or run, depending on the weather. These are recovery days so take it easy.

4. Once a week do a longer ride (perhaps two hours) or run (one hour).

5. On the seventh day rest.

I believe that a program like this has real potential for the time trial specialist. If you begin in mid-November and carry on through December, January and February, you will have built an excellent base of leg strength from the weights, overall body strength and some cardiovascular function from the circuit, anaerobic fitness from the ergometer, and aerobic fitness from the long ride or run each week. During March, April and May, continue doing the power workout once each week but eliminate the circuit and substitute one set of several upper body exercises similar to those I do mentioned above. Increase road miles, incorporate the usual speed work and retain the weekly long ride.

I would not be surprised to see a new breed of time trial specialist surfacing in the U.S. as these events, particularly from 10 to 25 miles, become more popular. These distances, with their premium on raw power, might best be prepared for in the weight room and on an ergometer in the off-season instead of slogging away on 100-mile rides in the snow. Some long-distance fitness will of course be sacrificed, but short-distance power should be impressive.

17
Annual Program
Achieve solid cycling fitness
by blending all the workout methods

HAVING JUST SOLD YOU on three training methods that can produce a fit rider and strong competitor, it is time to be bluntly honest: There is no magic in any of them. When it comes down to it, the magic is in the way that the divergent techniques of LSD and intervals and weight training can be blended and merged to create total cycling fitness. It isn't easy to do this, and the result is that many riders stick to just one training regimen. They may choose only LSD or only intervals because it is easier to go out and routinely pound away every day than it is to incorporate diverse methods into a comprehensive system. However, it is only through the judicious and balanced use of all three training techniques that you can become capable of performing at near your physical potential in all phases of the sport.

If you are a monomaniacal trainer, you will have only one strength in a race and that is rarely enough to do well. Like a one-crop economy hit by blight, failure in that specific area means you will have nothing to fall back on. Once again: You get good at those things you practice. The rider who trains doing only steady riding can get cooked when the action heats up, while the rider who trains using varied methods, including some intervals for speed development, is more likely to hold the pace. A wide range of training methods produces the ability to successfully handle a wide range of race situations.

The sound general plan for a good weekly training balance is to do one long, steady ride and two speed sessions (intervals, time trialing, motorpacing, actual racing), with the other days used for recuperative, short, easy rides or rest. And because balance is even more important on a long-term basis, each December is a good time to organize a training program for becoming a more complete and competitive rider throughout the season.

Of course, your ultimate accomplishments depend on many

factors. Included are your natural ability, the quality of your speed work, your opportunities to train and compete with top riders, and your mental commitment to excellence. But just as important, if not more so, is the aerobic base you develop before hard training and racing begins. A steadily increasing program of miles at a heart rate of about 130-150 beats per minute builds a base of aerobic function on which harder training can be done to advantage. Without this base, any gains from a more intense anaerobic program will be short-lived and subject you to the risk of severe breakdown. Therefore, any long-range training program must first place a premium on expanding your aerobic capacity.

Other considerations are your specific physical weaknesses and less-than-skillful riding techniques. The off-season is the best time to work on them. Once you have been racing or riding seriously for a year or more, you should have an accurate idea of your strengths and shortcomings on the bike. If you have speed but not the ability to last the distance, that deficiency has probably become painfully apparent during long training rides and races. If you are strong enough to finish the miles in good form but lack snap, you may have found out by doing much of the work for 50 miles only to see half the pack fly by in the final 200 meters. It doesn't take too many such experiences to figure out where you need improvement.

Similarly, you should establish some goals for the upcoming season. You may want to advance one category or place well in a certain race or simply keep up in rides with better cyclists. If so, you must have some sort of plan. Not everyone is goal-oriented, but progress in fitness and sports skills is rarely made without choosing some objectives, devising a reasonable method of reaching them, then carrying it out over a period of time.

You should also put off-season emphasis on increasing strength, as I discussed last chapter. Total body weight training, leg power development on the ergometer or squat rack, and the general muscular conditioning gained from participation in other sports all add to your base and determine how much you can improve.

With all this in mind, here is a sample yearly plan for the serious cyclist of any ability level. It is a suggestion, a rough outline rather than gospel, so adjust it to fit your own needs. The important thing is to have a definite program that suits your unique abilities and interests so that you won't be training aimlessly from day to day. But a word of caution: Don't do a specific workout just because it is on your schedule. If you feel tired or are getting sore, make an adjustment. As Eddy Merckx himself has said, blind allegiance to a rigid plan is a quick way to destroy both physical strength and your enthusiasm.

January and February

One day each week do a long aerobic workout. This can be on the bike, on foot, on cross-country skis or on rollers. This workout should last at least two hours at a heart rate of 140-150. Combine workout methods if you have to. For instance, if it is too cold to ride for more than an hour but your knees self-destruct when you run long, try riding for one hour, running for another hour and finishing up with 15 minutes on the ergometer or wind trainer.

Three days a week get in some endurance work at an easy pace or take part in an alternate sport such as basketball, skiing, handball or swimming.

Three days a week use weights in a circuit training workout and do some power work on the ergometer or a substitute like the Racer-Mate. Monitor your body. Weight training is intense and you should avoid workouts on consecutive days so that adequate recovery can take place.

During these two months, steadily increase the weight used in the circuit, the time and resistance on the ergometer or Racer-Mate, and the distance/time spent in aerobic development. For instance, a cyclist who begins light circuit training in December with one trip through the exercises will usually be able to increase sets to three, increase weight 30-50% and increase the speed and snap of the whole workout by February. If your long aerobic work is limited to running because of the weather, the 10-mile run you do at an 8-minute pace in December may increase to 15 or 20 miles at a 7:15 pace. (None of these figures are meant to be anything other than guides, of course.)

Your improvement depends on many factors, including how hard you work and how excited you are about increasing your performance for next season. But probably the most important factor is how bad you are to begin with. If you have never trained seriously before and are in miserable shape, you will progress drastically in the first few weeks. If you are already an experienced cyclist with several years of training behind you, improvement will come more slowly. Still, you will steadily develop strength and consolidate the base that your riding has given you.

During the winter you should also concentrate on correctable weaknesses. If you are too fat, this is the time to lose the extra

Don't let early season bad weather keep you off the roads. You need to learn to race under all kinds of conditions, as Bunki Bankaitis-Davis found in the 1986 world championships in Colorado in August.

weight (see chapter 8). If you need leg strength, adjust the circuit to include more intensive power exercises for the legs. If you can't spin smoothly at a high cadence, spend some time on the rollers and follow it up with low-gear work on the road. If bike handling is a problem, winter is a good time for some cyclocross.

March to early April

Get in a solid 6-8 weeks of increased miles. Cut circuit training to twice a week and go through it only once per session. Try to get out on the bike as much as possible. Ride most of the time at a brisk, steady pace but rarely go anaerobic. A Senior III with other responsibilities might work up to a ride of 30-40 miles on Tuesday and Thursday, 60-70 on Sunday, and 15-20 on the other days at an easier pace. This will allow for recuperation as well as aerobic benefits. The circuit work could be done on the short/easy days.

A building schedule such as this should ideally be increased each week by about five miles per ride, but most cyclists will find their progression halted by lack of time or daylight rather than by their endurance. It would be great to pedal 100 miles several times a week or go on long motorpaced rides, but few racers have the time.

Another problem at this time of year is weather. Just when you need big miles it is usually snowing or raining or both. Be mentally prepared to ride through anything. Get a rain cape, shoe covers and warm riding clothes. Maintain your bike between wet rides or get a second bike to use in the slop. During this period you should be trying to get outside on the bike rather than run or ride rollers. Given the vagaries of weather at many early season events, you need to learn to train in bad conditions because you will almost certainly get the chance to race in them.

About a month before the first race try to add some modest speed work, but don't overdo it. Airing yourself out with longer TT-type efforts is better than short, leg-searing interval training. Intense anaerobic work now will bring you to a peak too early in the season and may lead to injuries if done often in cold or wet conditions.

Mid-April through October

Tailor the bulk of the season to your own situation. You need to examine the racing calendar and choose the events you want to peak for. Identify others that you will ride for training, if that is your philosophy.

The theory is that you will reach a peak 6-8 weeks after beginning your interval program and then you can hold it for a slightly shorter period. While at your peak you can train hard, ride at your current maximum levels and recover quickly. But if you go too long doing anaerobic work, including racing, you will pass your peak and become overtrained. Your performance will deteriorate, you may lose weight and you will be unable to sleep — all signs of chronic fatigue. The only treatment then is to return to a program of moderate, steady miles to allow your system to regenerate. But if you can anticipate the end of your peak and shift to slow miles before you get stale, you can then ride aerobically for a month and produce a new peak period with better performances than before. If you don't anticipate the peak and instead drive yourself into deep fatigue, the drop in performance will be greater and the recovery period longer.

November and December

This is the off-season. It is the time for alternate activities that allow you to retain fitness but escape the onerous aspects of a rigid schedule and hard exertion. Don't plan a daily workout but do what you feel like each day. Ride a little, play some basketball, train in a low-key way for some running events, go backpacking, cross-country ski, or take up karate, soccer, dance or racquetball. Keep fit with varied and enjoyable activities each day.

18
Dear Diary

The most valuable training book
may be the one you write yourself

ONE PERSISTENT CLICHE which turns out to be true is that any training plan is only as good as the consistency and dedication with which it is applied.

In the simplicity of this statement it is easy to forget that you need some facts before you can train consistently. For instance, a six-week program of intervals is made much more useful if you can accurately determine what kind of improvement you got from all that sweat and heavy breathing. Otherwise you won't know whether to retain the regimen or modify it or forget it. In the same way you must be able to assess the benefits of a winter's weight training program to decide whether it is worth repeating during the next off-season.

Long-range planning for your training is virtually impossible without detailed record keeping that can remind you exactly what you did during a certain day, week or month and allow you to make judgments about its worth. The best way to be sure that such information is at hand when you need it is to keep a cycling diary.

Nearly every authority stresses the importance of a diary. The sport's traditional reference book, *Cycling*, published in Italy, suggests an elaborate record kept on a weekly card. USCF National Men's Coach Eddie Borysewicz speaks strongly in favor of training logs in his book *Bicycle Road Racing* and has shown the diaries of Polish stars Nowicki and Szurkowski at his clinics. Mary Jane Reoch, winner of numerous national championships, says she keeps detailed records. Bike shop owner Jerry Baker, who placed seventh in a National Time Trial Championship with a clocking of 57:25 when he was in his mid-30s, has recorded his miles since 1969.

Not all top riders follow the practice, or at least they didn't back in 1974 when a survey of national-class cyclists found that only 17 of the 28 kept records of their training. However, if Eddie B, based

A strong supporter of diary keeping is Eddie Borysewicz, men's road coach of the U.S. Cycling Federation. Eddie B says that most riders in his native Poland make a record of their training and racing, which gives them important information for setting up each season's program. A diary doesn't have to be elaborate. Just make sure it will hold up to constant use and that it provides enough room to record all the data important to your cycling program.

on his coaching and competitive experience in Poland, one of the world's stronger cycling nations, sees benefits in diary keeping for elite cyclists, it would seem to be just as important for everyone else serious about the sport. And it is especially vital for the beginning racer, who may not have the advice of a coach and is just starting the training which will shape his development in the sport.

Nearly all advantages of keeping a training diary derive from the comparisons it makes available. If you keep a record of your workouts from year to year, you can see the results of different training methods, dietary changes and equipment modifications. Let's look at some specific information the diary can give you and what you can learn from it.

Recording and analyzing data

One obvious advantage of record keeping is that you can chart your total miles for the year and for any period within it — the pre-season buildup from January to March, for instance. Compare this to your racing performances as the season wears on. Perhaps you'll find that more pre-season miles would give you the aerobic base to ride the early races more competitively while still retaining enthusiasm for later in the summer.

The most useful tool in evaluating mileage data is a graph. I have a homemade one with miles from 0 to 400 on the vertical leg and the weeks of the year on the horizontal. I chart bike miles in blue and off-season running miles in red. At the bottom, next to the appropriate week, I list top performances and notable disasters. I especially watch the curve of my buildup from January to April to see if I'm adding mileage too fast. Such graphs are fascinating over a period of years.

Diaries provide a way to judge the effects of endurance work other than cycling. For instance, you can determine the difference in your riding performance after a winter spent cross-country skiing compared to one spent running long distance, grunting through circuit training or sweating the cold weather away on rollers.

During the season, entries can reveal the change in racing performance due to high-intensity work like intervals or motorpacing. It is important to know how many weeks it takes to reach your peak through a given training regimen — say anaerobic sessions twice a week — so you can hit your top performance level for specific events in the future.

For example, by looking back over a period of several years you might see how doing intervals once a week brings you along slowly to a peak in about 12 weeks, while a schedule of three interval sessions per week gets you there in half the time. With a solid aerobic base and this information, you know exactly how long it will take to reach top form. But this can be calculated only if you've kept a record of past training and racing performances.

The data you accumulate will allow you to see the results of a winter weight program. Careful entries will let you know from one year to the next how many sets, reps and how much poundage you have used for each exercise. Comparing yearly race results helps you assess the value of specific exercises, as well as the relative benefits of different weight routines, such as circuit training versus a power program.

Training diaries are also a great place to record your race results. Put in the name of the event and starting time, the weather, the category you rode, your placing and time, along with the names of dedicated racers who finished ahead and behind. In this way you can compare your accomplishments in the same race from year to year and also see if you are improving or regressing in relation to other serious riders. You think you will remember results forever as you relive the competition after the event, but over the years the races will tend to run together in your mind. The diary never forgets.

Diaries let you analyze peaks and valleys in performance. You can do this through evaluation of race results or with periodic time trials. Once you have ridden either a PR (personal record) or what I wryly call a PD (personal disaster), you can look back at the preceding weeks and months to find out why it happened. In the case of great rides or a series of races in which you were consistently in top form, you can reproduce that preparation later.

Another valuable reason for keeping records is that you can track down the causes of injuries more easily. If you are having knee problems that cropped up for no apparent reason, an analysis of the diary may give you some clues. Did you change your shoes, cleat position or saddle height last month? How about that long ride two weeks ago? Maybe it irritated ligaments and you haven't recovered because, as the diary shows, you got inspired and rode 300 miles in the next six days with one race and two interval sessions. One thing diaries reveal in cold-hearted, objective and brutal style is the way we tend to get excited and overdo our training just when we are rounding into top form. Diaries mirror our ego, our stupidity, our unwillingness to accept our limits. Maybe that is why some racers don't keep them, and why those who do are often loath to act on what the records show so clearly.

Body weight fluctuations over a year or a career can also be charted. You can find out if you really do climb better when you are lighter or if you tend to lose some strength after your weight drops below a certain level. Knowing the poundage at which you function best is a great help in the struggle to achieve consistently good performances.

A diary allows you to see the effect that time of day has on training. If you have to ride for three months from 5:30 to 7:30 a.m. due to a change in your work or school schedule, you can compare the results of that routine to the afternoon workouts you're more accustomed to, particularly in relation to injuries. A current theory holds that your body is coldest and, therefore, more susceptible to injury early in the morning. Does this account for that bothersome tightness in your left thigh? A carefully kept record can help you figure it out.

Riders can present all sorts of reasons and excuses for not keeping a diary, even though they know it could help their cycling. Some can't remember to make daily entries. This problem can be conquered by keeping the diary on the nightstand and filling in the day's proceedings before going to sleep. Some riders stash their diaries in the bathroom next to the toilet paper and are able to make extremely regular entries. Or the diary can be kept near the bike's resting place and the data recorded upon return from each training ride. Any excuse for not writing down your workouts is just that — an excuse. If you really believe that keeping a diary can help you be a better rider, you will have no trouble remembering to fill it in.

There are some pitfalls of diary keeping, a main one being the recording of too much data and getting lost in trivial detail. You don't need graphs of daily caloric intake, a complete biorhythm chart, three pulse and blood pressure readings per day or a four-page narrative account of your mental processes during the ride. Just stick to a few important items.

Another danger some riders have encountered is the "diary miles syndrome." It is easy to get trapped in the belief that more miles equal better performance, the result being a constant struggle to make this week's total more than last week's, which was more than the week before that, and so on. For a while there is great satisfaction in the mere recording of these ever-larger totals, but the time will surely come when the physical and mental strain causes a breakdown. Don't let the diary become an end in itself; make it an aid, not a tyrant.

Information to enter

Here are some suggestions for actual entries. Although it looks like it will take you longer to write down the information than it took to do the workout, all these notations can be made in about three minutes a day.

Weight. Some riders weigh themselves every day under identical circumstances — before breakfast is standard — but I feel this is too frequent. Your actual weight won't fluctuate appreciably in 24 hours, although scale weight may vary as much as 5-8 pounds depending on your state of hydration. If you are training hard every day or riding a lengthy stage race, daily weight checks will help you determine if you are adequately replacing lost fluids. But during normal training, morning weigh-ins are unnecessary. Instead, step on the scale about once a week to check for any weight-loss trend. A steady decrease past your best racing weight may indicate that you are dipping into muscle reserves and in danger of falling victim to overtraining.

Heart Rate. This should be taken once a month — immediately after waking up is best — after you have trained long enough for your heart rate to stabilize. The newcomer to fitness will see his resting heart rate fall steadily during the initial months of training, from about 75 beats per minute in sedentary life to the low 50s as exercise strengthens the cardiovascular system and makes it more efficient. Once it reaches a stable rate (determined by heredity as well as training volume) there is usually no need to check it frequently. The exception is during periods of heavy training, especially when you are doing intervals. Then heart rate should be recorded daily because an increase (at rest) of more than five or six beats may be signaling the onset of staleness. Remember that a variation can be caused by so many factors that it is not a very reliable indicator of overtraining, though it certainly won't hurt to see if daily pulse checks have any predictive value for you. Here again the importance of recording exact figures over several years is obvious.

Workout. Record what you do on the bike each day. Note miles, route, gears and cadence, along with any special features of the ride, such as intervals, riding companions and weather conditions. Also include data on any timed sections. For example, I sometimes clock myself on a certain hill. This is not a scheduled time trial but I have gotten into the habit of jamming it in training. Over several years I've found that my time going up is an accurate gauge of my fitness. A sample entry reads: "Rode Olathe loop twice for 60 miles, done hard with a dozen jams on hills and flats. Coal Creek hill in 2:01."

New Factors. Make note of any special circumstances like saddle or handlebar height adjustments, new components or wheels, and clothing. For instance, unfamiliar shoes can cause knee trouble if the cleats vary the position of the foot on the pedal. Even if the resulting irritation is barely noticeable after one ride, the training diary helps you spot the pattern.

Evaluation. Include a brief subjective appraisal of how the ride felt. You could rate its quality A to F like school grades, or include a descriptive phrase: "Felt lousy first 20 miles — sleepy and heavy legs — but better during last 30." This entry is important because it helps you remember how your body and mind responded to riding on a given day, allowing you to more accurately assess the effects of previous days and weeks of training.

Stress Load. This pertains to things not related directly to cycling. Included are happenings in your off-the-bike life that can affect either training or racing performance, such as job or school stress, staying up late at night, illness and injuries, changes in diet, etc. Example: "54 miles — Ridgway and return — tired last 20 from bout with flu Monday. Felt okay rest of day."

Although the volume of information in my training diary helps me plan my workouts, it is a worthwhile journal for its own intrinsic merit. In the final analysis I need no excuses to justify keeping it. I like to browse through the entries I have made over the last 12 years, not to uncover any patterns but rather to re-experience the ride or race sketched out so sparely in terms of miles ridden, intervals completed and how the weather was. I keep a workout diary because it records an important part of each of the days of my life for reflection and remembrance.

19
Helmets
Hardshells are required for racing,
and recommended for training, too

I LIKE MY HEAD. Not that I have grandiose ideas of its comeliness, intelligence or general bearing, but I have found it to be a useful appendage that I could ill afford to lose. As a result I approach activities that pose a clear and present danger to my head with caution and what I hope is an adequate degree of healthy fear.

Still, I certainly don't avoid potentially dangerous situations. I enjoy mountaineering despite rockfall, downhill skiing though there is the chance of spills, and cycling regardless of the inherent tendency of two-wheeled vehicles to topple over. But I take precautions. When I ride the bike, that means wearing the best hardshell helmet I can buy.

In spite of that injunction, this is not going to be a holier-than-thou sermon about how I have never ridden without sufficient head protection. I understand the widespread resistance to plastic helmets among racing cyclists and have only recently begun to wear one in training. That decision, however, has caused me to examine the motives of cyclists in this controversy.

For example, the *Velo-news* issue that covered the 1978 World Championships featured a picture of Bob Cook, the late Colorado racer and Olympic team member. He was leading the pack up a hill and I had to look twice to identify him — he was wearing a leather strap helmet instead of the plastic shell he had used for so long that it had become his trademark. The reason for Cook's unexpected transformation was revealed a page later in an article that quoted a U.S. team mechanic: "(Cook is) a great guy and a good rider but (the coach) had to take him to one side and tell him to wear a proper helmet, a leather one. (The coach) told him you have to look like a European to ride like a European."

Cook had a reputation as a modest, self-effacing and intelligent young man. I understand the pressures brought to bear on top athletes by people who have authority in choosing national teams

There are many helmets on the market today that meet the standards required in USCF-sanctioned races. Though older photos in this book show amateurs in leather-strap helmets, that style became illegal in 1986. Lately even pros have been wearing hardshells in criteriums and other mass-start events.

and who, therefore, control an athlete's career. However, it is a pity that top racers are exposed to avoidable dangers for the sake of a theory that has no logical foundation whatever.

The longtime uproar about football injuries provides a comparison that strikes at the heart of the problem. For a number of years severe head and neck injuries were on the increase in that sport due to the prevalence of spearing and butt blocking techniques in which the head is rammed into the opponent. The helmet thus becomes an offensive weapon rather than a protective device. My own college football career took place when such tactics were popular and in the best Vince Lombardi tradition I, in my youthful naivete, practiced them eagerly. To strengthen my neck I did thousands of neck exercises, including heavy bench presses while in a wrestler's bridge, and blithely speared opponents for four years to the encouragement and approval of coaches and teammates. When I rammed someone with my heavy plastic helmet and metal face mask I felt like a real pro. The pressure on me to do so was greater than my fear of possible injury, even though the specter of paralysis frightens me more than any other mishap, or death itself.

The point is that in the milieu of violence encouraged by fans, coaches, players — people whose acceptance I most desired — I did not have the maturity or perspective to reject a dangerous technique.

In a similar way, the use of leather strap helmets in cycling is associated with high performance and the rider who wears something else is ostracized. Just as the football player looks like a real pro if he tackles with his head and face, so the cyclist wears a leather helmet to appear European and, therefore, competent.

The fallacy is obvious. In football there is no particular benefit to be gained in terms of performance by looking like a pro (spearing). A hard shoulder tackle knocks the runner down just as effectively but does so without also breaking three of his ribs. The object of the game is to tackle the runner, not maim him for life. Spearing is overkill. Similarly, in cycling there is no additional speed to be gained from looking like a European. Any reasonably comfortable helmet will allow maximum speed. You pedal with your legs, not your head, and any arguments about psychological advantages are just so many excuses.

That U.S. coach is right — you do have to look European to ride like one — but only if he keeps drilling that idea into the rider's head until the prophecy becomes self-fulfilling. On the other hand, the fact that it is only psychological means that it works in reverse. Sell the rider on the advantages of increased protection and he will ride faster wearing a plastic helmet because he will feel more secure.

The whole issue comes down to two factors. Vanity is the first. I have heard cyclists berate football as a violent game played by egocentric brutes who desire only to prove their masculinity. Yet these same riders train bareheaded because to wear hardshell protection seems to them unmanly. Such an attitude is irrational, counterproductive and ultimately courts disaster. Their attitude does not stem from intrinsic differences between cycling and football or any other sport; it arises out of similarities in human motivation regardless of the activity.

The second contributing factor is the patently ridiculous notion that on a physical level you must look European to ride like they do. Of course, the coach's comment may represent a minority view, but judging from the ratio of leather to plastic helmets at most U.S. races before 1986 I doubt it. Such a view is fraught with more logical pitfalls than can be adequately pointed out here. I agree that we should take advantage of the greater experience of European coaches and riders, but let's not blindly assume that it is the appearance of a rider that makes him fast or even accepted in top-flight racing circles. Plastic helmets don't seem to have slowed the march to superiority of the East Germans.

Many cyclists argue that the hardshell helmet is unnecessary for the experienced rider who can use superior bike-handling skills to avoid most crashes and minimize the results of others. This view is blindly naive. As an analogy, climbers classify rockfall and lightning as objective dangers, meaning that they are beyond human control. As such they are feared more than falls, which can be controlled by skill. But skill has little to say to the fact of rockfall, a rumbling affirmation of the climber's essential helplessness in the face of fate.

In the same way, the racer is at the mercy of the pack regardless of his bike-handling ability. If there is a crash directly in front, there is little that can be done. Errant cars pose the same kind of mindless, unpredictable hazard. It is only prudent to protect oneself against dangers for which skill alone will not suffice.

Risk is one of the attractions of many sports, and risks that arise out of the nature of the contest and that can be avoided with skill or with adequate artificial protection are acceptable. Risks that stem from the ego, or from peer pressure, or from the spectators' thirst for bloodshed are not.

What can be done? I dislike mandatory controls that restrict personal freedom and there is some validity to the view that a racer should be able to jeopardize his head if he wants to. I do not consider myself morally superior because I used to train wearing a cotton cap but have since converted. By choosing to wear a good helmet I am merely declaring that other considerations like style and conformity have become secondary in my hierarchy of values. Perhaps this decision is easier for me because I am not trying to make a national team. I do not deny any racer's right to wear the helmet of his choice as long as he is free to make that choice based on his own values at that time in his life.

Even with the helmet I may still sustain serious injuries if I go down hard or get hit by a car. No protective device is proof against all mishaps. But at least I am doing all that is technologically possible to prevent unnecessary head injury. That seems a large benefit from so simple an action as buckling on a hardshell helmet.

20
Skills & Tactics
Master these basic techniques
and you will be ready for racing

SKILL AND TACTICS play a much more important role in cycling than is generally thought by those outside the sport. To the uninitiated, a bike race looks like a confusion of activity with the best conditioned athlete winning. On the other hand, so much has been made of race tactics within the cycling fraternity that riders tend to overreact in the opposite direction and concern themselves too much with strategic maneuvers.

However, fancy moves are not of much use if you are a beginning racer. You need experience to see when they can be executed to advantage and you need the horsepower to bring them off. Make no mistake — most tactical moves depend primarily on riding strength. It does little good for a coach or team leader to tell you to go to the front on a climb, bridge a gap, or initiate a break with a quick burst of speed up the side of the road if you are barely hanging on. The first step to successful tactics is achieving an adequate level of fitness.

That said, it's also certain that you do need some skills to race successfully even at the beginning level. Cycling is just as much a skill sport as baseball or handball, with the added penalty of a possible crash if you don't execute properly. With this in mind, let's look at some basic techniques that every serious cyclist should know before even attempting to compete. Once these are perfected, you can move on to poring over European race accounts for the latest winning ploy.

The art of the start
We may as well begin at the beginning: You have to get your foot in the pedal when the gun goes off. Although this seems so elementary as to be unworthy of mention, nearly every Senior IV mass-start race, especially early in the season, seems to feature a pileup. When the gun goes off, someone inevitably fumbles around trying to get his foot in and six other riders crash in their

attempts to avoid him. Such disasters aren't unknown among more experienced riders, either. There was a revealing photo of the start of the women's World Road Championship several years ago in which a member of the British team was obviously having this very problem.

The solution is simply to practice the gentle flick of the toe that levers the pedal into position for the shoe to slide in and the cleat to engage. This is true whether you use traditional pedals or the newer step-in models. In race situations, pedal a few strokes to match the speed of those around you before reaching down quickly and snugging the strap. If you have deeply grooved cleats it may be unnecessary to tighten up except for a sprint or a hard climb, especially if you've adjusted the strap so your shoe goes in without leaving much slack. Practice your pedal entry every time you ride and you'll be confident for the race.

Sometimes a few equipment modifications are helpful for ensuring a trouble-free start. See to it that your pedals have a tab on the back of the cage. Even inexpensive models now seem to have this feature, which gives your toe something to turn the pedal over with. If yours don't, consider either replacing them or attaching, with epoxy, a makeshift metal tab. Another workable solution on a cheap pedal is a short bolt that protrudes in the same manner as a tab. Put it through a reflector hole on the back of the cage. Also helpful is a thin piece of rubber glued to the shoe in front of the cleat. It prevents the smooth sole from slipping on the metal as you try to toe the pedal over.

Riding a straight line

A second simple but necessary skill is riding a straight line. Beginners are notorious for their inability to do this, but some extremely fast and experienced racers are also guilty. The reasons are a lack of skill on the part of the novice and a lack of concentration or concern by the hotshot, but the results are the same: The undisciplined rider wastes energy and poses a danger to everyone else.

Practice for this skill consists mainly of concentrating on holding your line during training rides. When you are riding alone, put your wheel on the white line along the edge of the road and try to keep it there. You'll find that success isn't a matter of steering the bike in a straight line but of having a relaxed upper body and a light touch on the handlebars. When out with another cyclist, ride shoulder to shoulder so that you learn to bump elbows or knuckles without flinching. Develop a pedal stroke that eliminates the side-to-side motion which can make you weave erratically.

Above all, be predictable. Close pack riding demands that everyone be on the same wavelength. There must be a basic understanding of what is and is not expected behavior in a given circumstance. Even though Senior I-II races are faster, they are often safer simply because the riders have enough experience to behave more uniformly than IIIs and IVs.

Following a wheel

At race speeds it is estimated that drafting another rider saves you about 15% in energy output. Therefore, it is foolish to be out in the wind continuously unless you are going it alone for some good reason or unlucky circumstance.

Ride with other people to perfect your ability to follow closely with safety. Keep your front wheel about a foot behind the one you are following, soft pedaling when necessary to maintain correct spacing. Try not to use your brakes. Doing so will slow you more than needed and a too-large gap will open, creating chain reaction-type problems for those behind you. When a gap does open, be careful that you don't make things worse by accelerating too hard, overrunning the wheel in front and grabbing the brakes again, thus starting the process anew. If you don't become proficient at following a wheel, you can waste more energy than you save by constant yo-yoing.

One of the best ways to practice this fine art of wheelsucking is to do some two- or three-person team time trials where a premium is placed on the ability to smoothly sit in. If you have no riding companions, pacing behind a small motorcycle will help and also give you a good workout. Don't put all your attention on the wheel immediately ahead but keep an eye out for obstacles in the road and changing terrain. When looking past the front rider your peripheral vision will let you know where your wheel is in relation to his.

When working in a paceline, don't accelerate when it is your turn at the front. The idea is to maintain the group's speed as the lead rider pulls off; he drops to the back not because you go faster but because he decelerates slightly. After your own bout against the wind, pull off to the side agreed upon and stay close to the others as you slide back. This enhances the drafting effect for the whole group and keeps everyone as far out of the traffic flow as possible, making paceline riding possible even on busier roads. As you come abreast of the last rider in the line, pick up speed and then slide over to his wheel as he comes past. When done correctly you won't need an energy-wasting acceleration in order to latch back on. Once in the caboose position you can take a drink, adjust a toe strap, rearrange your shorts, stand to stretch, etc. without disrupting the smoothness of the paceline or posing a danger to your companions.

Pack riding

When surrounded by others a primary objective must be the protection of your front wheel. If your rear wheel is struck a fall is unlikely because it has nothing to do with steering the bike. However, if your front wheel is contacted it will often be twisted off line faster than you can react and you will almost certainly go down. Help prevent this by never overlapping your front wheel with someone else's rear. If that rider switches abruptly for any reason, he'll feel nothing but a bump as you are sent to the pavement.

Use your hands to fend off riders who encroach into the sacred space surrounding your front end. Practice reaching out with either hand while training alone. When with a companion, reach over and touch his bike and body until you can do it and still ride straight yourself. When overtaking a rider it is accepted practice to touch him lightly on the hip so he knows where you are.

Try to ride near the front of the pack. The back would seem to be the easiest place because of the greater draft, but there are major drawbacks. In the rear you are out of touch with what is actually going on in the race — up front is where the action is. Also, if someone crashes directly ahead you can get taken down or at least be slowed considerably while you pick your way through the wreckage. Riders in front of the crash will instinctively accelerate when they hear it happen and you may not see them again until the award ceremony.

Corners are especially tough for the back-of-the-pack rider due to the so-called accordion effect. Because lead riders can pick the best line, they are able to go through a corner at optimum speed and then sprint away. The bulk of the pack must go at slower and slower speeds as the glut of riders funnels into and then out of the turn.

The ideal situation is to be among the front 10 or so riders. If you are caught at the back you can move up by being alert for openings. When one develops, fill it quickly and smoothly. Good riders can get their bikes through any opening big enough for the

Group training is the best way to get used to riding close to others. If you practice bumping shoulders, elbows and hands you will be much more confident in race packs.

handlebars, but beginners should be a little more cautious. Another avenue to the front is to follow an experienced rider as he threads his way through the maze.

Good bike handlers will sometimes go up the gutter or onto the gravel shoulder to improve their position, but this can be dangerous if the edge of the pavement is raised or there is glass and other debris. If you do try this technique it pays to look ahead for obstacles. I have seen a racer take to the gravel and accelerate right into one of those green metal mileage posts.

In races not closed to traffic, the left side of the road makes a poor route to the front. Not only do you chance being penalized or disqualified for crossing the center line, you also run the considerable risk of meeting a car. It is easy to get stuck out there in the left lane like a pilot fish beside a shark, not strong enough to get all the way to the front and unable to find an opening in the picket fence of elbows. No race is important enough to risk becoming a hood ornament.

Cornering

Corners are the novice bike handler's nightmare. Part of it is the increased danger — most crashes take place in corners. Also,

Alex Stieda and Rigobert Matt illustrate just how far a bike can be heeled in a turn. Note their excellent technique: weight on outside pedal, knee slightly bent, butt on rear of saddle, brake levers released. The ability to corner like this comes with experience that produces confidence in bike-handling skills — and in the effectiveness of rim cement.

poor cornering technique can put you off the back in a hurry if you go through slower than more experienced competitors. California cycling personality Nik Farac-Ban, a former Veteran national champion who didn't start racing until he was in his 30s, once commented that in his first events he was strong enough, but due to inexperience he cornered badly, lost a little ground on each turn and eventually went off the back.

Novices aren't the only riders who can benefit by working on their cornering. Internationally, the Colombians are noted for their climbing ability but one of their aces, Antonio Londono, ingloriously lost his overall lead in the 1980 Coors Classic due primarily to poor cornering. Jonathan Boyer lapped him three times and gained back more than four minutes in the last stage of the race, a 50-mile criterium with several 90-degree corners and an

S-turn. According to Boyer, the Colombians were known to have trouble in turns and he and his team exploited this deficiency to snatch the individual championship.

The basics of cornering are simple: Approach the turn from the outside, choose your line and dive through. For instance, as the racing pack approaches a 90-degree right-hand turn, riders will jockey for position on the left side of the road so they have more room for the maneuver and can take the corner at maximum speed. Be prepared for this movement. If you get caught inside, be ready to fend off riders coming down on you from the left or you may get pushed off the road.

Once you have leaned the bike over, you are committed to your line. If you try to change it abruptly to avoid a rock, pothole or other rider, you may crash or cause others to. By the same token, it can mean disaster to hit the brakes when you are laid over in a turn. Enter it at the correct speed and accelerate coming out. There seems to be some validity to the theory that the bike will go where you look, so focus your attention on the spot where you want to emerge from the turn, not on the threatening curb.

When in the corner, have the outside pedal down and your weight on it, but keep the knee slightly bent. This gets your center of gravity low and ensures maximum tire adhesion. Don't fight the bike; let it sweep through the corner. Sitting on the back of the saddle helps increase rear wheel traction and adds stability in case the pavement is slippery or there is sand or gravel. Some riders will tell you to stick your inside knee into the turn, contending that this accentuates the weight shift, lowers the center of gravity even more and catches air to temper speed. I have mixed feelings about it; in a tight pack the advantages may be offset by the danger of contacting another rider.

Be ready to use your hands to ward off or hold up another rider who is encroaching on your line. It is possible to get a shoulder under a rider who is losing it and who threatens to take you down as well. In this and other crowded situations, don't tense up. Relax so you can absorb shocks and respond to the fast-changing situation. Because lead riders know that racers at the back will be slowed by the accordion effect, they will fly through the corner and jam out hoping to establish a gap. Be prepared by riding near the front and be ready to get out of the saddle and go. Poor technique here can really hurt. If you have to sprint out of every corner to catch the pack, you won't last long. A 40-mile criterium around a rectangular, one-mile course means you have to take 160

Once out of the turn, lead riders can sprint to high speed as those behind are still slowing to funnel through. That's the so-called accordion effect.

corners. Unless you can handle 160 intervals, you'd better make sure you are in a smooth groove near the head of the action.

Practice cornering alone and in groups every chance you get. The streets in residential neighborhoods make a good place to hone your technique. Don't forget that turns come in two directions, and always make sure your tires are glued on securely and are up to proper pressure.

Climbing

Climbing is very important in racing, but it is not so much a skill as a demonstration of superior heredity. If you have a good power-to-weight ratio you can probably climb well. If you don't, there are several things you can do to improve what nature has provided.

Lose weight if you need to get rid of excess fat or muscle, particularly in the upper body. I did not realize how important this was until I rode the Bob Cook Memorial Mt. Evans Hill Climb, a 28-mile ascent on the highest paved road in the world. The first time, as a 165-pound Senior III with 9.5% fat, I placed sixth. A year later, at 150 and 8%, I won that category. I am too big-boned and mesomorphic to be a natural climber, but this experience showed me that a great deal of personal climbing improvement is possible through weight loss alone.

Be sure you have proper gearing for the course. Many riders

tend to gear too high, then are forced to stand up while their pedal cadence drops to 60 and their efficiency drops to zero. I usually sit on longer climbs and pedal a little lower gear at higher r.p.m., but it really depends on individual preference. Choose your gearing to suit your technique. If you like to alternate sitting and standing, realize that each time you get off the saddle the effect is to throw your bike backwards several inches. When riding alone this is of little consequence, but when someone is close behind it could cause your rear wheel to hit his front and cause a crash. The solution is to pull the bike under you as you rise from the saddle and resist making a heavy lunge on the first standing pedal stroke. It takes some practice but it will make you a safer rider to be around.

Riding form on hills should reflect the more muscular effort. When sitting, pull on the bars to give the legs something to oppose. Keep your hands wide on the tops to facilitate breathing. A moderately bobbing upper body, something to avoid normally, is a natural and permissible way to help keep a steady pedal rhythm. When off the saddle and working hard, lean your bike from side to side so that each downward stroke can receive the direct weight of your body. Make sure, however, that this flip-flopping doesn't cause you to ride all over the road; for the sake of safety and efficiency maintain as straight a forward path as possible. You will probably have the best control if you grip the bars wide using the brake lever hoods. During any climbing, make maximum use of your cleats and straps to claw the pedals around.

The usual advice to a poor climber is to get to the front of the pack or even break away as the hill approaches. This is intended to allow the rider to climb at his own pace, drop slowly back through the pack as the ascent progresses, but still be in contact at the top. This seldom works for novice racers, however. Usually riders don't climb well because they lack fitness, so advice to attack before the hill is like telling them to improve their climbing by climbing faster. If you don't have the horsepower to climb, you probably don't have the strength to achieve the most advantageous position before the ascent. Good climbing is less a matter of skill than of power and fitness.

Descending is another matter. Here skill and experience are everything. You should try to pedal downhill because this increases your stability, assuming you have a smooth stroke at high cadence. When you get spun out, squeeze the top tube between your knees to help dampen any shimmy that could result in loss of control. Corner with the same technique as on the flat — weight back, outside pedal down, center of gravity low.

Climb in the manner that gets you over the top best. On short "sprinters'" hills most riders find this to be off the saddle all the way, with hands on brake lever hoods. By rhythmically leaning the bike side to side, each pedal can receive a direct thrust of leg strength and body weight.

When there is a series of downhill turns, you must think ahead in order to set up for the next one and then the one after that. Fast, safe descending requires practice, experience and a finely tuned kinesthetic sense. Sometimes it comes down to how much you are willing to risk. Mike Neel's solo victory in the Boulder Mountain Road Race stage of the 1980 Coors Classic, gained on his hair-raising descent of South St. Vrain Canyon, was that kind of ride.

Sprinting

If you are strong and skillful enough to arrive at the finish either with the pack or in a break, your ability to sprint will decide whether you finish at the top of the results or as an also-ran.

Some riders are natural sprinters. They usually have a fairly high percentage of so-called fast-twitch muscle fibers which give them above average leg speed, and they have a fast reaction time. Both of these components of successful sprinting are largely inherited and cannot be changed appreciably by training. If you aren't blessed with the basic ingredients, you can strengthen your quadriceps so you can go faster by handling a larger gear. Weight work and big-gear training sprints will help, though there is a limit to the improvement possible. Bike racing has been called more a speed sport than a power sport. Big-gear work can turn your legs into lactic acid factories and your sprint into a plod while faster riders spin by.

There are some tactics that will help you take maximum advantage of your natural ability. In the mile just before the sprint, look for a strong rider and get on his wheel. He may take you into good position and you can then gamble on slingshotting around him in the final 100 meters. Remember that everyone else is looking for that leadout, too, so you will have to fight for a good position. In the actual sprint, concentration is essential. Sprinting is a painful, anaerobic effort that usually comes after several hours of hard exertion. The rider who can make himself work at top capacity in spite of the pain is more likely to win.

You can start your final sprint by getting out of the saddle, but many road sprints are more like long windups that bring everyone to near maximum speed, making a track sprinter's jump unnecessary. A technique that may help you break through your personal speed limit is to concentrate on "pedal faster" rather than "pedal harder." Some riders, especially those who lack natural talent in sprinting, find that this emphasis on increasing r.p.m. — trying to make the feet fly around no matter how big the gear — yields better results than if they approach it as a muscular, pushing effort.

Pulling hard on the bars gives your legs something to brace against. A good weight training program will provide the upper body strength necessary to use this technique. Bent rows are a particularly good exercise because they simulate the actual riding position. Squats will develop power in the quadriceps and lower back.

Stay alert when sprinting. Don't just put your head down and go for it. Although a straight line is the fastest route to the finish as well as the safest, you can't count on everyone sprinting this way.

Practice sprinting in group rides. Choose certain road signs or landmarks and go. The only way to get the feel of road sprinting is to work on it. If you train alone it's tougher. I often practice my technique by riding on a wide, moderately traveled road and sprinting against cars that overtake me, but this is useless for learning tactics.

Once sprinting and the other basic skills are learned and your

Davis Phinney's road sprint is one of the best in U.S. cycling, and he proved it when he became the first American to win a road stage of the Tour de France.

experience in time trialing has given you the ability to bridge gaps and attack on your own, you will be ready to move on to more advanced race strategy.

You needn't have the technical know-how of former national team mechanic Steve Bishop to perform basic maintenance on your bike. Most riders don't mind the weekly 30-45 minutes it takes to clean, adjust, and lubricate a bike. Simple, routine procedures will keep the machinery looking good and working well, and it can catch a problem that might otherwise leave you stranded far from home.

all your minor position adjustments. Because of a bike-rending crash in a criterium, I once had to buy a new frame the day before the District Time Trial Championship. Although the dimensions of the replacement were identical to the one that had deceased, it felt different. I was not comfortable with it during the TT and my disrupted concentration kept me from riding my best. There are enough things to think about in a race without worrying about the bike.

In the same way, decide several months in advance on component choices like chainwheel size, brakes and brake pads, and the saddle. Above all, don't hesitate to ride a new bike in all kinds of weather before the first race. A rider I know got a new Italian superbike in February several years ago but was so afraid of

21
Final
Preparations

Make race days less hectic
by getting ready well in advance

THE HOUR OR TWO before a race can be a hectic and perplexing time because there is so much to do amid so much confusion. You have to pump up tires and assemble your bike, checking derailleur and brake adjustments in case anything got bumped in transport. Getting registered is often frustratingly slow because at some races it seems like those in charge are either late or disorganized or both, and they never have change when you pay your fee. You have to get dressed, pin on numbers and locate a restroom. Then you must find a place to warm up among hordes of other cyclists of all classes, ages and abilities.

All this necessary trivia is made more difficult by that sinking feeling in your stomach, that sense of anxiety and the dry mouth that mean your system is readying itself for the stress ahead. With all the sound and fury of a race, it pays to complete as many of the preparations as you can well in advance.

Many riders devote the evening before a race to final mechanical adjustments, and it is true that this is a good time for checking last-minute details. But real race preparation begins days and weeks before the actual contest. The better you take care of the small details early, the less you will have to worry about during the frenetic pre-race hour and the smaller will be the chance of major problems. Let's look at some specific ways to make your pre-race preparation as efficient as possible.

Early decisions

Make your equipment decisions months before the competitive season starts in order to have time to become fully familiar with every component. If you are going to get a new bike or frame, do it early so you can accustom yourself to its handling and work out sullying the paint or getting grime in the bearings that he trained on it only when the roads were dry. Sure enough, it rained on the day of the first race and he crashed in a corner because he had no feeling for how the bike handled on wet pavement.

Advance maintenance

If you will be using a trusted old bike to race, complete all bearing maintenance at least a month in advance. This is especially important for the bottom bracket because when you replace crank arms after repacking the bearings they sometimes work loose. Each arm must be checked periodically and perhaps retightened for several hundred miles. If one comes loose during a race it can easily be ruined; it will slop on the axle and destroy the close tolerances necessary for a correct fit.

The headset adjustment is also precise and it'll take a number of miles to see if you (or the shop) did it correctly. A headset that comes loose can lead to poor handling and shimmy at high speeds, as well as scoring and pitting in the bearing races.

Be sure to mount your competition tires on your racing wheels in time to ride a couple hundred miles on them prior to the first race. This will assure that the tires are not defective, that they seat properly and that the glue is sufficient. Nothing is more disheartening than to roll a tire and crash, unless it is to fail the bike inspection before you ever turn a pedal in anger.

Pre-race week

All equipment should be given a final going-over during the week leading to the race. If the event is Saturday I suggest making Thursday your day off from training, using it to do final mechanical work. Some riders train right through early season races, but I think a day off two days before an event is important physically and mentally.

Use the respite from riding to first clean the bike thoroughly. Hose down the frame, scrub it with soapy water and a brush, and wipe it dry. Use a rag and rubbing alcohol or a household cleaner to remove stubborn splotches. Then put on the racing wheels, install the freewheel and chain you use for competition, and adjust derailleurs and brakes.

The racing components will already be clean and lubricated if you make it a practice to maintain them after each event before reinstalling training equipment. Use a solvent such as kerosene (gasoline is too harsh) or a water-soluble auto engine degreaser and a toothbrush to clean the chain and derailleur jockey wheels. This can be done with the chain removed or right on the bike by taking out the rear wheel and letting the slack chain hang in a shallow pan of solvent. While you are at it, scrub the chainwheel teeth and front derailleur. Use a rag, shoeshine fashion, to clean the freewheel cogs. Then apply the appropriate bicycle speciality lubricants to the chain, brake and derailleur pivot points, and the freewheel bearings. This maintenance should also be done to training equipment about once a week all season.

Don't forget to pack spare wheels for the race. Most riders use their regular training wheels as back-ups. Be sure the rear wheels are identical in terms of dishing and freewheel position on the hub so there will be no difficulties with brake and derailleur adjustments. Tom Sain is a rider who can attest to the importance of this. He punctured just before his start in 1980 National Time Trial Championship and the replacement wheel was incompatible with his bike. He rode away from the line to the sound of grinding metal, losing the chance to defend his U.S. record against Tom Doughty's challenge on the fast Bisbee, Arizona course.

At road races, be sure to Magic Marker your name on your spare wheels if they are to be kept in a common wheel van or even in a team car. Incidentally, spare wheels are a good idea even if you are an unattached rider with no support vehicle. If you should puncture during the warm-up you will be able to change the wheel and not miss the race.

Gather all the tools you will need. Check the adjoining list and be sure to add anything you may need for your particular components. You won't have time to do anything major just before the race, but if you have prepared your bike properly you won't have to. An assortment of tools will allow you to make minor adjustments on the spot. Running around trying to borrow a T-wrench five minutes before the start doesn't help your race concentration.

On the day before the race go for a short ride to test the bike and loosen your legs. Pedal briskly in low gears most of the ride but run through the whole gear sequence to be sure the derailleurs are adjusted properly. Carry along a small screwdriver in case they aren't. Try several short, hard sprints to check for chain skip. If everything works well, you can confidently put aside the mechanical aspect and turn full attention to other final preparations.

Don't race in clothing that you have never trained in. New shorts can cause severe abrasions if the chamois has seams in unfamiliar locations or if the fit allows the legs to ride up. New

shoes are another problem because cleats can have subtle alignment differences that won't show up in a short pre-race warm-up
but may cause knee pain and ligament trouble during a hard ride.
Also, new shoes may require repositioning of the toe clips or even
installation of a different size.

The day you use to clean and adjust equipment is also the time
to go over your race clothing. Polish your shoes, replace laces as
needed and make sure cleats are tightened securely. If you have a
permanent number, pin it on your jersey. Assemble clothes for the
race, including warmups and items like leg warmers that you may
need if the weather turns out to be bad. Go over the checklist to be
sure you haven't forgotten anything.

To shave or not to shave?

A continuing controversy concerns the pre-race ritual of shaving off leg hair. Many riders of both sexes and nearly all top-level
racers do it as a matter of course. The advantages are that shaved
legs are easier to massage, abrasions from a fall will be less severe
(especially, some say, if the skin is lubricated with an ointment)
and risk of infection is lowered because a wound can be more easily
cleaned, medicated and bandaged. In addition, vanity is certainly
a factor — as any bodybuilder knows, muscular definition and
vascularity stand out more vividly when the skin's surface is
hairless.

But there are some definite drawbacks. If you are a male, the
first shave will be a tedious, inch-by-inch process as the razor
constantly clogs with thick hair. Try clippers first, then tackle the
resulting stubble with a razor. Once finished, the sensation of
having bare legs may be so unsettling that you will lose sleep,
literally, as the sheets touch your skin as never before. With this
possibility in mind, it would be wise not to have the initial shave
on the eve of a race but a week or so before.

Also, some people have sensitive skin and frequent shaving
might irritate tender hair follicles, creating the same sort of
potentially dangerous infection which shaving is supposed to
prevent. At the least, shaving legs every week is time consuming
and bothersome.

One other point to consider: Male riders with shaved legs run
the risk of hearing some pointed comments about their sexual
preferences. The community you live in makes all the difference in
this respect. During a summer in Boulder, a laid-back and liberal
community, I never felt awkward about shaved legs. Boulderites
are so used to strange behavior and extraordinary sights that a

man with hairless legs is beneath comment or notice. However, I live in Montrose, a small community 250 miles and about 10 years removed from the Boulder-Denver area. For that reason it is a great place to live, but my neighbors know nothing about cycling and its arcane customs.

I think shaving should be a personal decision. If you feel comfortable and more hygienic with hairless legs, do it. But if you feel strange about shaving, there is no cycling rule that says you must. In fact, there is a backlash; in some circles it is fashionable for even top riders to go *au naturel*. This assumes that shaved legs are the result of vanity alone and rejects the whole custom. As we have seen, there are other reasons for shaving down and it's certainly the custom in European cycling, but you obviously don't need such cosmetic tinkering to ride fast.

Fueling up

Proper diet, too, begins months before the first race. As discussed in chapters 7 and 8, I feel that a moderate, balanced selection of food will ensure an adequate supply of vitamins and other essential nutrients. If you wish to lower your percent of body fat in an attempt to improve performance, start in the off-season so any strength loss from cutting calories won't interfere with your in-season training.

During heavy workouts in the weeks before the race be sure to eat enough to fuel your long rides, but don't overdo it. It is possible to add useless fat even when you are training hard. In fact, there are accounts of European pros who gained weight during the Tour de France.

The most important nutritional rule the week before the race is to not change eating habits. Dietary manipulation could upset your system and add yet another stress to the normal tensions. If your training has been going well you obviously have been eating properly, so why change for the race?

The much-ballyhooed technique of carbohydrate loading is an example of a drastic change in diet that usually doesn't work, especially when it is applied in its strictest form. Despite all theoretical benefits, the depletion stage plays havoc with the body and mind, and the loading phase causes weight gain and muscle tightness due to the water bound up with the increased glycogen stores. Most top riders don't load to any extent beyond simply making sure they eat a good variety of carbohydrate-rich foods in the days before a race. Because they deplete glycogen almost every day with training rides of two hours or longer, their muscles need constant energy replenishment in the form of carbohydrates. Upsetting the normal eating pattern will almost certainly cause problems.

It's best to have the biggest carbohydrate meal two nights before the race so that it will have plenty of time to be stored in the muscles in the form of glycogen. Spaghetti, a noodle dish or several baked potatoes with vegetables and bread are all good choices. Some riders like pancakes topped with sliced peaches instead of syrup. On the eve of the event, avoid spicy or unusual foods so your stomach won't be upset. More than one racer, tempted by the fiery menu at a Mexican restaurant, has spent half the race looking for roadside bushes.

Riders are divided on the subject of eating on race day. Some like to ride shorter races on an empty stomach, believing that it makes them lean and mean. This is a personal matter and you will have to experiment. However, most riders like to eat something if the race starts late enough in the day to make it practical. The general rule is to eat at least three hours before a road race, four hours before a criterium and five hours before a time trial. In other words, the more an event calls for immediate exertion, the less you want in your stomach.

During longer races you will need to eat something to stave off the dreaded bonk, an extreme state of fatigue caused by the depletion of glycogen in the muscles and liver. Your extended training rides will tell you how long you can go before experiencing the danger signals of weakness, light-headedness, tunnel vision and black spots. Once the bonk's got you, you've had it, so avoidance is the key.

Anti-bonk measures begin with eating enough carbohydrates during the two days before the race to ensure a high glycogen level. During races which will last longer than about two hours, begin eating and drinking early. Slices of peeled apple, grapes, banana, orange, etc. are ideal. Unless race food is wet, small and easy to swallow, you'll never get it down. Don't be misled by the stories of European pros eating their cheese sandwiches, rice and sugar squares, and other solid food. They may be able to do this in the early and middle miles of their six-hour road races, but don't you try it in the typical Senior III-IV 40-mile road race.

Fluid replacement is also important, and controversial. In times past it was customary for racers to take along one bottle of water (approximately 20 ounces) in events of up to 50 miles, two for those lasting longer. In training they might not take any water at all, the theory being that this would somehow condition them to

Riders in the Tour de France often do 200km stages for days on end and they know the value of eating and drinking during a race. For any event longer than about two hours, take along plenty of your favorite liquid and some easy-to-swallow food.

do fine without it. However, it now appears that nothing could be further from the truth. As Dr. Ed Burke points out in *Inside the Cyclist*, "It is not unusual to lose 5-10 pounds of water (a pound equals one pint) during a two-hour bicycle race. As a consequence, rectal temperatures may rise to 105 F degrees. This overheating and dehydration place severe demands on circulation while reducing exercise capacity and exposing the cyclist to various health hazards (heat exhaustion and heat stroke)."

Especially in temperatures of 80 F degrees or hotter and when humidity is high — in other words, typical conditions during much of the U.S. racing season — fluid replacement during training and competition is vital. Burke flatly states, "Any rider who starts a road race in hot weather with less than two water bottles is only limiting his performance." Further, "The rider who trains without fluids thinking he is producing a lowered need is making a foolish mistake. Make a conscious effort to drink 4-5 ounces every 10-15 minutes in hot weather training and racing." Burke also recommends drinking 13-20 ounces about 15 minutes before starting out.

Given the importance of fluid replacement, what's the best thing to drink? Plain water is close to ideal, seeing as how it is quickly absorbed by the system and it constitutes the great percentage of what perspiration is. Water can also be used as a refreshing douse for the head, neck and legs (don't try it with Gatorade). As for the many commercial replacement drinks, their primary marketing angle is that they replenish electrolytes (sodium chloride, potassium, magnesium) and help restore muscle energy. The former is of questionable benefit, according to Burke, since "the body has such a vast store of (electrolytes) that even loss of several pounds of water will not deplete its supply. . . A cyclist eating a well-balanced diet should be able to compensate for electrolyte losses. . . ." Still, it might be good insurance to use a replacement drink in the heat of the season, perhaps not carrying it on rides but simply having a tall glass before and/or after each workout.

However, beware if the drink contains some form of sugar as a means of replenishing energy, especially if you would carry it in your bottles during training and racing. Burke reports that "the addition of even small amounts (of sugar) can drastically impair the rate of stomach emptying. Anything above a 2% solution (one tablespoon per water bottle) will reduce the rate at which water leaves the stomach; and remember, water is what the body needs immediately. As carbohydrate supplementation during exercise is of secondary importance anyway, the sugar content of drinks should be minimal."

Go ahead and try various fluids — plain water, sugared water, diluted fruit juice, tea, a commercial concoction like ERG, etc.— and see what agrees with you. But do all the experimenting in training, not out on the race course where you want to minimize surprises. And, as Burke says, when you find something that works well remember to drink it often.

I usually pack my race rations in an ice chest to keep them fresh. I include extra water and more fruit for after the event. Since quite a few road races are out in the country far from stores, it can be a long wait from the time you cross the finish line until all riders are in and prizes are awarded.

At the race site

If all these preparations have been faithfully observed, you won't have extraneous details cluttering up your concentration when you arrive at the race. Register immediately so you are then free to get the bike ready, dress and begin warming up. If it is a

During the middle of your pre-race warm-up, get off the bike and do a few stretching/limbering exercises.

short course that you haven't seen before, ride around it easily to loosen up, making note of terrain and road conditions. Also take a good look at the finishing stretch and pick out a landmark that lets you know when you are within 300 meters of the line.

The shorter and faster the race will be, the more important the warm-up. For a time trial, for instance, your body should be completely ready for a maximum effort right from the start. In a long road race or one with several neutral miles at the beginning, you don't need as much. In general, warm up by spinning steadily in low gears until you are loose and perspiring. Get off the bike and stretch, then do some speed buildups over 200-300 meters. Finish with a couple of short sprints.

Schedule the warm-up so you will have about five minutes before the start in which to compose yourself, regain normal breathing and concentrate on the task at hand. Save your socializing for afterwards. Too much pre-race chatter diverts your attention and wastes the energy you should be channeling into competition. You've trained hard, so make the most of each racing opportunity by being fully prepared.

Pre-Race Checklist

EQUIPMENT

- [ ] Bike
- [ ] Spare bike
- [ ] Spare wheels
- [ ] Frame pump
- [ ] Spare tire
- [ ] Bottles
- [ ] Wheel covers
- [ ] Food and drink for race
- [ ] Race instructions (location, time, etc.)
- [ ] Racing license
- [ ] Toilet paper
- [ ] Blanket
- [ ] Money
- [ ] Alcohol and washcloth
- [ ] Rub and towel
- [ ] Lubricant for chamois
- [ ] Thin plastic sheet and/or paper for insulation

TOOLS

- [ ] Floor pump and adapter
- [ ] Tire pressure gauge
- [ ] Spare adjustable cleats
- [ ] Adjustable wrench
- [ ] Screwdrivers
- [ ] Lubricants
- [ ] Rim glue
- [ ] Spoke wrench
- [ ] Freewheel remover
- [ ] Chain breaker
- [ ] Extra freewheel or spare cogs
- [ ] Allen keys for stem, etc.
- [ ] Saddle spanner
- [ ] Special tools for your components
- [ ] Waterless hand cleaner
- [ ] Clean rags

CLOTHES

- [ ] Helmet
- [ ] Cotton cap and/or sweatband
- [ ] Number
- [ ] Jersey
- [ ] Wool or cotton T-shirt
- [ ] Shorts
- [ ] Suspenders
- [ ] Socks
- [ ] Shoes
- [ ] Gloves
- [ ] Leg warmers and/or tights
- [ ] Show covers
- [ ] Arm warmers or long-sleeve jersey
- [ ] Windbreaker

22
Time Trialing
*A race against the clock
is the perfect event for beginners*

QUITE A FEW experienced road racers profess that they hate time trials. They say the excitement of mass-start events is missing: no strategy, no teamwork, no tactics. In some cases this distaste is mental. Compared to time trialing, it is psychologically easier to ride a mass-start race because you are too busy thinking about strategy, position in the pack, and avoiding a crash to dwell for long on how badly you are hurting. A TT, on the other hand, requires that you concentrate intensely on your pain and discomfort so that you can go at your maximum speed for the distance.

It is perhaps due to a quirk in my character that I like time trials very much. For me their fascination arises from the fact that I must tread on the edge all the time — the anaerobic threshold, the fine line between lightness and durability in equipment, and the mental line that defines just how hard I can push myself. As I see it, the time trial is the event for the limit-seeker, the rider who accepts personal challenge and enjoys meeting it in the toughest arena there is: the battlefield of one's self. The ideal effort will put you on the red line of your capabilities where it is physically painful and mentally excruciating.

There are no excuses in a time trial. Road racing results, however, are frequently influenced by luck or by factors other than one's own power and fitness. Crashes, wheelsucking, the refusal of some riders to work in a break — all these and more have been offered as reasons why the strongest rider sometimes doesn't win. But time trials have no place for alibis. Barring a puncture, it's just your fitness and your will against the unyielding clock. No wonder Europeans call time trials the "race of truth."

An event for everyone
Because of the nature of the event, a time trial is the perfect medium for exposing riders of all ages to cycling competition. If

you are fascinated by racing and want to try it, you don't need an expensive bike to ride TTs because you can compete against yourself, against your previous best time. You don't need to be accomplished at drafting, riding elbow to elbow, sprinting, and all the other road techniques that take time to learn. Since such skills must be practiced in the company of others, time trialing is a natural choice for the cyclist who lives far from population centers and cannot often train in a group.

Time trials are an ideal way to gauge your strength and improvement. The objectivity of the clock lets you see the state of your fitness and evaluate the effectiveness of your training. Without the benefit of time trialing, some prospective racers never make it to the line because they are unsure if they have the speed and endurance to stay with a pack. Others try sanctioned events before they have a sufficient mileage base, get dropped or suffer inordinately, and never race again. Time trials let you compare yourself with racers in your category so you can see if you're ready to take the plunge or if more training is needed.

Once you have started racing, good time trial results against riders in the next higher category may help you decide whether to advance. Quite a few riders qualify through their race placings to move up, but they are hesitant to do so. If your TT results are comparable to those who would be your new opposition, there is a good chance you can advance and be competitive.

The chances of accident in a time trial are small. It is rare to crash unless you take the turnaround too fast or blot out everything but the mesmerizing spin of the front wheel and ride right off the road. A time trial is the safest way to introduce new racers to the thrill of going fast on a bike.

However, one danger a time trialist does face is vehicular traffic, a common enemy in all open-road events. This point was sadly underscored by Alan Kingsbery's nearly fatal collision with a cement truck going through an intersection during the 1978 National Championship. A time trialist must take on the difficult responsibility of riding alertly even as all resources are being thrown into going fast. Whether you are competing in a TT, a mass-start event, or are simply out training, you have to ride defensively and with awareness.

Importance to road racers
Time trials are a valuable training technique for a rider at any stage of development who is interested in road and criterium racing. In order to ride a time trial at maximum speed, you have to

train your body to operate at its anaerobic threshold. This is the level of exertion where you are working so hard that the slightest increase in effort would cause more lactic acid to accumulate than your system can eliminate. It is exercise at the brink. When the anaerobic threshold is crossed, the body's response is to slow down almost immediately.

On the anaerobic threshold is precisely where you are during a time trial. The value of this is indicated by Dr. Ed Burke, who says, "Your potential to be a successful endurance cyclist appears to be related to your anaerobic threshold." Another physiologist, Dr. Ben Londeree, says, "A significant portion of training should be done at a pace which exceeds your current anaerobic threshold." An excellent way to achieve this is to ride time trials of 10 miles or less at a faster pace than you could sustain for 25, approximately the USCF championship distance. This sort of training will make you a better time trialist and will also improve your motor for road racing.

In addition to general fitness, time trialing develops specific road race skills. If you're a strong solo rider you are better equipped to get back in the pack after a crash or a puncture. You will also be able to bridge a gap to a break without needing half the pack to help. Finally, TT ability may allow you to get away and stay away for long periods. Unless you have a devastating sprint, an escape based on time trialing power may be the best chance you'll have to win.

Equipment modifications

Time trialing is the last refuge of the hard-core equipment freak and many riders make drastic modifications in favor of lightness, but this can be carried too far. It is alluring to think that an ounce saved here and a bit of rolling resistance eliminated there will result in significantly lower times. It won't. You may save a few seconds with some judicious weight paring, but going overboard may lead to equipment failure. Light wheels and tires are an example. You can save some rotating weight by using a radially laced 24-spoke front wheel, a 28-spoke rear, and 170-gram tires, but the price you pay for the ounces saved (besides what the cash register demands) is a greater likelihood of punctures and wheel malfunctions.

In the same way the search for component and frame lightness is often counterproductive. A very light frame may flex so much that the advantage of weight reduction is negated by its absorption of your energy. Drilled cranksets are visually impressive but

*More than one road race has been stolen by a strong time trialist who was allowed
to escape early and then was never seen again. A well-timed solo break can also
work late in the race and is worth a try if several strong sprinters are still in
contention.*

also may flex too much. The result of an obsessive search for
lightness looks great on the scales but often loses its luster on the
road. Unless you are going for broke in the Worlds or have the
money, time and inclination to tinker with titanium frames and
gossamer tires, I suggest that you use your regular road bike for
time trials. All your training miles have accustomed you to how it
rides and your correct position has been established. These
advantages will be negated to some degree if you try to do a
maximum effort on a rigged-up TT special that just doesn't feel
the same. You also have less chance of punctures if you ride your
standard racing wheels and tires, such as low-flange 32-spoke
hubs, rims of 310-350 grams, and 250-gram tires.

Not to be overlooked is the fact that you won't have to spend
the time necessary to modify your equipment when each TT comes
up. Time for the sport is better spent riding the bike than
tinkering with it. Besides, there is a certain ego boost in performing well without relying on light equipment to help you do it.
But if you want to make some simple weight-reducing modifications, hoping for either a mechanical or psychological advantage,
there is a moderate approach that avoids most of the potential
problems. I don't necessarily recommend it, but the following
might help your performance on a flat course: Remove the inner

chainring, front derailleur and its lever and cable. Take off the bottle cage, pump, and spare tire. Clean the grease out of each hub and replace it with light oil. Don't use a freewheel with cogs larger than you'll need.

Some riders move the saddle to the rear, arguing that this gives them increased leverage and the ability to push a bigger gear. Personally, I am against alterations in normal riding position. You should find your most efficient position long before you compete. Any sudden changes, when combined with the stress of pedaling in big gears, are likely to produce knee injuries rather than fantastic times.

Advising the use of "tire savers" in a time trial is probably heretical, but I suggest that you consider it. They really do help prevent punctures while adding virtually no weight or rolling resistance if adjusted to barely brush the tread. If you suspect the TT course may have glass, thorns, or other debris, using these simple lightweight gizmos might save you a frustrating puncture. If you don't finish, you can't win.

Like many cyclists, I rode my fastest 25 miles — 58:27 in the 1978 Colorado district championship — on an unmodified road bike. It had heavy rims, 250-gram tires, tire savers, a bottle cage — the works. Yes, I might have gone faster on a lighter bike. But on the other hand I might have punctured, had an equipment failure, or had my painfully generated horsepower sucked up by a whippy frame or drilled-out components.

Actually, the biggest detriment to speed in a time trial is air resistance. You can help counter it by wearing a snug jersey tucked into your shorts and by taping the vent holes in your helmet. Some advantage may be gained by using a sleek one-piece skin suit. Former national 25-mile record holder Tom Doughty swears he feels faster in one, but it takes a lot more than tight clothes to ride a 52:25.

Physical preparation

Physical preparation for time trials starts months before the event and differs little from the training routine that any road rider follows. The basis for top performance on the bike, regardless of event, is the long-term development of solid aerobic ability based on one long steady ride each week in addition to other training.

Remember, however, that if you are going to specialize in time trials of 10-25 miles, you don't need the 100-mile rides or 400-mile weeks of Senior I road racers. This is one reason why TTs are ideal events for those who have other responsibilities; you can still compete successfully without spending great amounts of time in training, and the simple addition of one other longer ride each week will give you the stamina to compete in road races as well as longer time trials.

In addition to an aerobic base the time trialist needs power. You can develop this through a weight training program like the one I described in chapter 16. During the racing season don't neglect a maintenance program of one set of several basic exercises done to momentary muscular failure two or three times a week. This takes only a few minutes at the end of a training ride and helps you keep the muscle gained during periods of intensive strength training.

Training races

As the weather improves and the first competition of the season approaches, increase your mileage and focus on specific routines designed to develop time trialing ability. Foremost among these are training TTs.

Locate courses 3-10 miles in length on your normal training routes. A smooth road with little traffic and no stop signals is best. The fewer intersecting roads, the safer you will be. Don't be afraid of some rolling hills but avoid sustained climbs. It helps if the courses are a good warm-up away — five miles is the minimum distance to ride before making a hard effort; 10 is better.

Once a week ride a training time trial to your current physical limits — all out, nose to the bars, guts on the road. As the first race nears, increase the distance of the effort. This level of intensity can be hard to muster, so get other riders involved if possible and make these training time trials into competitive events. This is the sort of function that clubs are perfect for. If you have to go it alone, get keyed up and be prepared to suffer. Once a week you can usually summon the psych you need, but more-frequent repeats often come off half-heartedly. Going all out once a week is better than making three lackadaisical efforts.

Mentally, it helps some riders to schedule a certain day for their training TTs. They write it down in their workout plans, note it on their desk calendars, eat a light breakfast on the appointed day, and generally make a big deal out of it. During the ride they carefully check their intermediate and final times and scrupulously log these and things like temperature and wind conditions. Others prefer to forget all about it until, halfway into a ride, the spirit moves them and they rocket off from where they are to that white house three miles down the road. Either method can work, but it is important to ride the same route occasionally so you can compare times and see if your training is producing results.

When time trialing (training or racing) it is important to maintain an aerodynamic riding position. It is tempting to sit up during a TT effort in order to breathe easier or because your back is aching, but you will learn to pedal in an efficient position and become accustomed to it only through experience. If you allow yourself to let up in training, you will want to do it in a race where it can make a critical difference. For example, a rider of my acquaintance refused herself the luxury of standing to rearrange her uncomfortable shorts during a USCF 25-mile district championship. When the results went up she was the winner — by *one* second.

Ways to build speed

Beyond the longish time trial done once a week to get used to sustained efforts, you can ride a series of shorter, interval-type of the repeats in the middle of the sequence so you can check your progress. This sort of training can be done during rides of 25-40 produce an oxygen debt. They are important because if you can go 32 m.p.h. for a mile, it is easier to go 26 m.p.h. for 25 miles. Intervals develop a top end. They also have the advantage of being easier to tolerate mentally, thanks to the periodic breaks.

TT interval training should emphasize longer periods of exertion — about two to four minutes — than interval workouts for road racing. Use a lower gear than you would in competition, keep cadence above 100, and pace each effort so you go anaerobic only during the last 15 or 20 seconds. Between efforts roll easily in a lower gear until your heart rate comes down to 100-120, then go again. You can also do these intervals on an out-and-back course, one mile each way, so you get specific practice on the start and turnaround. Don't let your cadence drop during the "on" segment; you have to learn to pedal smoothly during maximum effort. Start with no more than three of these intervals during early season workouts, then raise the number and the gearing as the season progresses. Do them on the ergometer if the weather is bad. It is good to note the time between two landmarks during one of the repeats in the middle of the sequence so you can check your progress. This sort of training can be done during rides of 25-40 miles. Combined with aerobic pedaling, these intervals will help build stamina as well as speed.

Gimmicky as it sounds to some riders, an electronic speedometer with a cadence counter, like the Pacer 2000, is a useful tool for monitoring efforts in TT training. If you begin by riding a three-mile course at, say, 23 m.p.h., the speedo will show your improvements in speed week by week. In addition, it will immediately indicate when your cadence is slowing. This helps you learn to keep a consistent pace for the duration of the effort.

Many top time trialists swear by motorpacing for training. It does work well, but I don't recommend it for novice riders because it is dangerous and illegal, at least technically. A good substitute is riding at high speed on a long, gradual downgrade, or with a blustery spring wind at your back. The effect of both is nearly the same as motorpacing, but there is one drawback to the latter method — that head-down grind into the hurricane to get back home. At least it builds power.

Franz Hammer, several times National Veteran TT Champion, says the best way to get in shape for time trialing is to ride long road races. The effect of hours spent in a fast pack is similar to motorpacing. Adding support to this is the fact that the winners of most important time trials are not specialists but good road riders who feel at home in a big gear for long periods of time.

TT racing

Several days prior to an important time trial be sure that any equipment modifications you have made work properly. At least by the day before, set up the bike exactly as you'll be racing it and take a short ride. Do some jumps in the gears you expect to use most so you can check for chain skip. This is extremely important if you are matching a freewheel and chain not normally used together, or if one of the components is new and the other has some wear on it.

On the morning of the race avoid food unless there is time to eat a very light meal, such as toast, several hours before the start. If your stomach isn't virtually empty at the start, it may be five miles down the road. The exception is for longer events like a 100-mile or 12-hour TT where the initial level of exertion is not so extreme and you will need the food energy as the ride progresses. For 10- or 25-mile events, however, your energy will come from the food you eat and the rest you get in the days leading up to the race, not from anything you do in the preceding 12-24 hours.

Some racers prefer not to ride at all the day before an event; others will simply go short and easy, testing the bike and loosening their legs. Experience will tell what works best for you. The important thing is to arrive at the starting line with a high level of physical and mental energy. Trying to cram in some eleventh-hour training is a sure way to prevent an optimum performance. Put trust in the weeks of preparation you've done. Your rising reserve of strength and the normal nervous energy that precedes competition may make for a fitful night's sleep on the eve of the race, but don't be too concerned. Experts say, and experience seems to prove, that the quality of rest two nights prior to an event is considerably more important than that which is gained (or missed) the night before.

Warm-up is critical

Get to the race early enough to register and have time for a good warm-up. Unless your muscles and cardiovascular system are ready to go at 100% effort from the start, you will lose time in the first mile or so. Also, trying to ride at maximum speed when the body isn't ready will drive you deep into oxygen debt. The buildup of lactic acid will be difficult to eliminate and your efficiency later in the race will be hampered.

Warm up for a 25-mile TT by riding about 10 miles. Increase gears and cadence as you begin to feel comfortable. When you are loose and perspiring freely, do a couple of short, hard sprints alternated with half-mile buildups to competition speed and gearing. All of this should be scheduled to end within five minutes of your start time, allowing you to roll easily to the staging area and catch your breath but not cool down.

During the warm-up be prepared for eventualities. Have spare wheels handy in case you puncture before your start. It pays to think through some strategies to deal with the unexpected. Beth Heiden had a bad moment at the 1980 Nationals when her rain-softened shoes made it difficult to engage her cleats at the start. Such a freak circumstance is certainly difficult to foresee, but you can be assured that if something can go wrong, it will.

The start

During your training leading up to the race be sure to have practiced the start. This comes automatically if you have the opportunity to compete in club TTs; if not, ask a friend to hold you in position as you make several attempts. If you are by yourself, roll almost to a stop and then jump. You need to know what gear to use and how to get underway without wobbling down the road and losing valuable seconds. Having done it a few times will increase your ability and confidence.

When leaving the starting line, strive to keep the bike stable and on a straight course while standing to build speed. Get off the saddle after every shift until a strong rhythm has been established in the primary gear. Pictured is Kent Bostick who won the individual and team time trial gold medals in the 1985 National Championships.

When your minuteman leaves, roll up to the line in your starting gear. The holder will grasp your bike, allowing you to reach down and make sure your toe straps are tightened just right and shoelaces are tucked away. Put your right-hand crank arm at the 2 o'clock position, ready to receive your initial downward lunge. Then relax and empty your mind of all thoughts except positive ones about the race ahead. Several deep breaths are calming and they serve to prevent the shallow panting that gives you a system full of carbon dioxide, but don't overdo it. The timer will keep you advised of the number of seconds remaining, then begin a countdown of 5-4-3-2-1-GO! On about "3" squeeze one or both brake levers and rise off the saddle. On "1" release the brake as well as your energy. And off you go.

Stay out of the saddle until you reach top cadence in your starting gear. Then sit down, shift, stand to build speed quickly, sit down, shift into your primary gear, stand briefly to get it rolling, and settle into your rhythm. From there on out it's going to hurt. If it isn't tough you aren't going as fast as you could. If you are fit and in good form you will perceive the pain as effort rather than agony. If the pain is not almost more than you can tolerate, bear down harder. Alan Kingsbery said that after the painful first miles he felt like he was "joy riding," but most riders I talk with share my perceptions — you have to suffer all the way to succeed.

Gear selection

Don't overgear. There is a tendency among some U.S. riders to use outsized gears like 53x12 when they can't handle them. Even if they can initially keep their cadence above 90, their style goes to pieces under the strain, leading to premature fatigue. Be wary of the attitude that equates big gears with macho. The correct gear for a time trial is the one that you can handle for the distance. Just because Greg LeMond or Ron Kiefel uses a certain ratio is no reason you should. In fact, it is a clear indication that you probably shouldn't.

Even though the trend is to bigger gears, the secret is to find the cadence at which you are most efficient and then select gears accordingly. Few studies have been done to determine optimum cadence and their results vary widely, indicating that it is probably a highly personal thing. There is some evidence, not surprisingly, that you are more efficient at the cadence in which you train, so time trials should not be ridden at r.p.m. appreciably lower than your training rate. It follows, then, that you should train at a brisk cadence so you can go faster in competition. I am more a pusher than a spinner but I like to stay near 100 r.p.m. A big gear is no cure for deficient fitness and style.

The mental aspect

Once you have done your training, a TT is 90% mental. Given equal physical ability, the rider who can concentrate best will win. Force your mind on the pain and effort or it will certainly wander and you will slow down. Only through an act of will can you keep your body operating at peak efficiency.

Sports psychologist William Morgan argues that there are two types of mental approach to athletics. The dissociative rider ignores the pain by allowing his mind to wander to pleasant thoughts during the event. He may mentally build complete houses or chant mantras as an escape mechanism. The associative athlete, on the other hand, concentrates fiercely on the pain itself — the burning lungs and aching thighs. Morgan postulates that this latter approach is the one used by the successful competitor. It produces the continual monitoring of performance necessary for reaching the upper limits.

It comes down to this: If concentration wanders, you will back off to a more comfortable pace as your mind quite understandably tries to ease the pain. Racing is an unnatural act, so you can't blame your mind — it is only trying to avoid some agony; it doesn't believe that you really want to hurt yourself so badly. If you try to ignore the pain it will go away, but so will your chances for success. A tenet of Zen belief is that those things you fear should be embraced. A great fascination of time trials is that they make you mentally turn around and confront your pain honestly.

Racing techniques

When the course has short hills try to keep your big gear turning. Stand up and roll over them instead of shifting down. You may incur oxygen debt doing this but it can be overcome on the downhill. Only experience will tell how far past your anaerobic threshold you can go and still recover. Keeping your momentum is a key to good results. Ride in the trough where the right-hand wheels of cars travel. This is usually the smoothest part of the road and is less likely to have puncture-causing debris. This will also put you far enough from the edge of the road so that you are free to concentrate on power output, not bike handling.

Keep your hands on the drops and pull on the bars so your legs have something to oppose, but don't grip so tightly that you lock the muscles in your arms and shoulders. If you have established an aerodynamic riding position in training, you will be able to get your back and upper body into the pedal stroke. However, this doesn't mean you should be bobbing and weaving on the bike. A little movement is unavoidable when you are using a big gear, but keep it to a minimum or you will waste energy.

Breathe from the belly. Don't fill your lungs, fill your diaphragm. Avoid the rapid, shallow breathing that doesn't efficiently eliminate carbon dioxide. This is another facet of hard riding that requires strict attention.

Use cyclists in front of you for a psychological boost, a target to shoot for. The ideal situation is to have a minuteman you can catch just before the turnaround, and another rider who can serve as a goal in the mentally difficult third quarter of the race. It rarely works out so perfectly, however, and often you will be pedaling the whole way in the gap between two other riders, or being sucked up by those who are faster.

Time trialing is an individual contest, so convince yourself before the race that what others do isn't going to affect your resolve to ride your best. I confess, though, that the sight of a rider ahead but within reach gives me that little extra — a mental set that has been conditioned by a competitive sports background. The ideal time trialist would ride to 100% of his ability regardless of outside stimuli.

Vehicular traffic on a TT course is a mixed blessing. Because you have to be alert for cars and trucks, a nose-to-the-stem riding style is definitely not recommended. On the plus side, vehicles passing from behind create a vacuum effect that helps pull you along. It isn't drafting and it isn't illegal; in fact, some of the fastest times ever recorded have come on heavily traveled highways. Britain's legendary time trialist, Alf Engers, cracked 50 minutes for 25 miles several years ago but he was accused of riding too far out in the lane, backing up traffic and virtually motorpacing a whole string of passing cars to the new record.

Most U.S. time trials are held on sparsely traveled roads, but even infrequent traffic passing from behind can help reduce your time. On the other hand, oncoming cars can slow you down, especially when the road is narrow. The rule is to accelerate whenever you see or hear a car. If it is coming at you, you will have to go faster to get through the wave of air without losing speed. If it is approaching from the rear, increase cadence as it begins to pass and you should be able to maintain a faster speed for quite a while without much risk of oxygen debt.

As you approach the turnaround wait until the last moment to shift into a lower gear and sit up and brake, thus maintaining your speed as long as possible. Resist the urge to soft pedal with 50 meters still to go, although you do have to give yourself enough time to check for traffic coming up from behind. Ride on the far right side of the road to create the maximum width in which to circle the traffic cone — practice this in training so you can shave it closely. Then get out of the saddle and get up to speed again, using a similar technique as at the start, regaining your primary gear as quickly as possible. It pays to push a little over the edge here because the slowing at the turnaround can rob your momentum and ruin your rhythm.

Wind is the time trialist's worst enemy. If an unfavorable wind is consistent, choose a lower gear that allows the proper cadence and then ignore the gale. A tougher situation is a gusting wind that keeps you from getting into a regular rhythm. You may have to shift often to maintain your best cadence, but don't curse the wind. Instead, concentrate on your riding and do the best you can. Remember that everyone else is fighting it too.

A tailwind is a blessing only if you have a gear big enough to keep a strong cadence without spinning out. Even here concentration is important. It is easy to work so hard on the headwind leg that you ease up going back and actually lose some time despite nature's help. But the worst situation is having a tailwind on the way out and a gusting headwind on the return. Such adversities are one reason why the event is called a trial.

As you reach the last quarter of the ride try to increase your effort. Here is where you can take a chance on blowing up. Even if you do and have to slow down, you are close enough to the line that you can usually tough it out without losing too much time. On the other hand, you gain valuable seconds if you pull it off. When you can reach the line at full speed and yet feel unable to hold it for another pedal stroke, you have apportioned your energy correctly.

After finishing cool down by rolling around in a low gear until your breathing returns to normal and your legs recover; if you get right off the bike you will be much more stiff and sore the next day. Put on your warmups and ride some more, or at least do some walking so blood circulation in the legs is maintained and muscles and knees won't tighten up.

The next day spin easily and don't be in too much of a hurry to resume hard training. This short break allows your body a chance to recover from the stress, and it gives you a little time to bask in the accomplishment of your ride.

Finally, evaluate that accomplishment. Reride the race in your mind and decide what went right and what went wrong. Identify your weaknesses, the things that cost you time, and work on them in training. But do this in terms of your own potential, not in relation to the results of others. Time trials are for the challenge of improving your performance. There will always be someone who is faster, but only one person can break your personal record. Doing so is cause for celebration, never dismay.

23
Criteriums

Skill in America's No. 1 event
will improve all of your racing

IF YOU ARE going to be a successful rider, you need to get good at criteriums. Most U.S. events aren't long and grueling road races or lonely time trials but fast and flashy whirls around several downtown blocks. Because of this, a road rider without a strong sprint can get pretty discouraged. Even weekend stage races usually feature at least one criterium, meaning that to do well in general classification you have to hold your own on a tight-and-fast course.

Although many riders and coaches say that America's criterium-heavy schedule works against the development of strong roadmen for international competition, it can't be denied that criteriums have their own special magic for riders and spectators alike. The racing is exciting because the frequent corners make it seem as if you are moving even faster than you are. A criterium on an intricate course blends the background into a blur; the individual sounds of spectators become a smooth sheen of noise.

Criteriums introduce an element that is missing from most other events — a crowd. Enthusiastic spectators can motivate a rider to perform in a way he didn't think was possible. Short-course ace Davis Phinney, for example, said that one reason he won the North Boulder Park stage of the '82 Coors Classic was the vigorous vocal support of his hometown fans. At times it seemed that he was being carried around the course on a crescendo of cheers.

Learning how to ride criteriums will improve your skills for road racing. Circuit road races are often held on three- or four-mile loops with sharp turns and narrow pavement. Criterium racing is perfect practice for them. The speed, snap, and sprint that you'll develop won't hurt regardless of the road course profile.

Time trial specialists can benefit, too, since they often neglect high-cadence speed work. Criteriums can put snap back in the legs after miles of big-gear training. And don't forget that not all time

Speed and bike handling are the skills essential to do well in criterium racing. These short-course events are popular with crowds and provide an excellent training ground for track and road racing.

trial courses are flat and straight. Taking the fastest line through corners is as much a prerequisite for victory in some races against the clock as it is in a crowded criterium.

Finally, criteriums develop bike-handling ability. Even if you enter only an occasional time trial and don't think that you need the skill and reactions necessary to ride in a big group, remember that you train in traffic every day. Criterium racing can make you a safer cyclist.

Criterium skills

Exactly what skills do you need to become a good criterium rider? Speed is obviously high on the list. If you are a powerful rider who lacks snap, you won't win many criteriums. You may be tough on the hills and devastating in time trials, but if you can't jump hard out of corner after corner, close gaps quickly, and still go like a scalded cat in the final sprint, you'll be doomed to frustration.

In fact, speed is so critical and yet possessed by so few riders that it has given rise to the theory of the "born sprinter": Either you can sprint or you will never be able to. This discourages some riders to the point where they avoid criteriums as well as speed training. But as with most either-or statements, the truth probably lies somewhere in the middle. Of course criterium success is more likely if you have natural speed. But if you are lacking, don't give up. There are ways to improve what speed you do have, and good strategic skills are just as important as sheer acceleration.

Begin your quest for speed by using a winter weight program to develop explosive power. The stronger you are, the more effectively you can use a big gear. Squats, leg extensions, and leg curls are obvious exercises but don't neglect your upper body. If arms, shoulders, and back aren't strong enough to stabilize your body and bike in a sprint, you'll waste precious speed in side-to-side movement.

Speed also can be developed by using an ergometer or Racer-Mate, TurboTrainer, etc. You need to pedal against high resistance at a fairly low cadence (around 90) to develop strength, but you should also make 30-second all-out efforts in the highest resistance you can handle at 120-150 r.p.m. High-cadence work on the rollers is beneficial too. Rollers don't supply the resistance of ergometer-type equipment, but a lot of sprints are won by someone who can spin faster than his opponents. Roller racing, a winter activity popular in some parts of the country, is a good way to develop suppleness at high pedal speeds.

Once you begin outside riding use a low fixed gear — 42x19 or 18 — to help accentuate a round pedal style and fast cadence. This will carry over to your competitive efforts later. It is traditional in Europe to accumulate the first few hundred miles of a road season in a fixed gear, but this has been slow to catch on in the U.S.

Whether you ride a fixed gear or not, stress high cadence from the beginning. For example, jam at 150 r.p.m. down shallow hills to develop leg speed. This will also keep you from blowing away your knees against big-gear resistance. But a word of caution: Though low gears will save your patellar tendons (the location of the knee injury most often associated with cycling), if you don't gradually work up to fast spinning you may strain the ligaments at the back of the knee.

Once you are conditioned it's good to agree on a gear restriction when training with other riders. This will keep things interesting and within reason in those sprints for city limit signs, mailboxes, etc. Also establish some ground rules. Will sprints be no-holds-barred, simulating competition? Or will you go side-by-side trying to match cadence? Knowing what to expect may prevent mishaps.

When the racing season begins, do some speed training at least once a week. This should not be confused with interval training. The purpose of intervals is to develop recovery and endurance by beginning each hard effort before you have fully rested from the previous one. But when working on speed you must allow your breathing and pulse to return to near-normal levels between the efforts.

Once a week do five or six wind-up sprints of about 400 meters. Start with a steady buildup of speed over the first half, then put everything into the last 200 meters. Between efforts roll easily and recover sufficiently to keep top-end speed and r.p.m. high. If you begin to slow down from fatigue you are doing endurance work, not building speed.

Check your progress by timing the last 200 meters. You and a training partner can time for each other, or strap your watch to the handlebars. Start it before the buildup and note what it says as you enter the 200-meter all-out zone and as you leave it. Record the information in your diary.

Of course, one of the best ways to build speed is to compete in track events if you are fortunate to have a velodrome nearby.

Bike handling

The other prerequisite for successful criterium racing is a large arsenal of bike-handling skills.

When I first decided to compete, I had never seen a bike race. I figured I'd better watch one to find out for sure what I was getting into. I ended up at a Senior I-II criterium in Colorado Springs. The sight of all those racers going through the corners so fast and so close together almost ended my plans right there. I wondered why a 30-year-old needed to do this. What perverse quirk of my mental make-up had whispered in my ear that bike racing might be fun?

In spite of my fear I did begin racing, of course. And I learned quickly that the bike handling that makes criterium riding safe and enjoyable isn't acquired by magic but results from plenty of specific practice. Most established riders have picked up their skills in actual competition over the years, but the beginner usually goes into his first criterium on a wing and a prayer. This probably explains the high incidence of crashes in Senior IV events (and maybe the fairly low rate of license renewals).

Like most other seeming obstacles, the bike-handling requirements of criteriums also represent opportunity. On a flat course tight turns are the best place to get away. Fast, sure lines and strong jumps out of each corner by the front riders can quickly break up the bunch. Unfortunately, too few novice riders belong to a club that offers a minimum three-part introduction to criterium racing: instruction, specific drills, and practice with other riders in competitive situations. Most prospective racers are lucky to get exposed to even one of these before they find themselves hurtling toward the first turn with 50 other equally nervous and un-prepared beginners.

No newcomer has the criterium skills of a Davis Phinney, but with practice they can be developed. A good all-round rider feels at home on the bike. He can do a trackstand at a traffic light, ride smoothly over curbs, jump potholes and railroad tracks at high speed, and keep the bike upright when the rear wheel skids in a turn. He can pedal easily with his arm draped over the shoulder of another rider, offering congratulations or condolences. He can reach out to hold up a rider who is leaning into him. When the worst happens he knows how to fall so he incurs minimum damage to his body and his bike. Then he knows how to get back up quickly and use the surge of adrenaline to fuel his chase back to the bunch. All these skills can be learned through practice.

Most riders train on smooth roads with few corners. They tend to ride fairly slowly through the turns because of traffic, pedestrians, etc. As a result they get little practice cornering at high speed or riding tricky road surfaces. It shows in their race performance.

Practice program

I suggest a three-part program beginning in the off-season to help you improve criterium bike-handling skills.

First, develop your general agility and reactions by devoting some time to body-awareness sports. At a USCF clinic, track coach Carl Leusenkamp told me how top cyclists are using gymnastic drills and tumbling. Downhill skiing, soccer, basketball — any sport that requires your left foot to know what your right hand is doing will help. There are some pretty poor athletes out there on bikes, at least from the standpoint of eye-hand coordination and kinesthetic sense. A rider who hasn't mastered patting his head and rubbing his stomach at the same time won't be a bike-handling whiz.

Second, do some off-pavement riding. Get out and do it in the dirt (or mud, sand, snow) several times a week. You don't need a fancy cyclocross or mountain bike. I use an old racing frame with inexpensive components and a pair of bombproof clincher wheels. About a mile from home there are fields laced with dirt roads where I can chase prairie dogs and jump over sagebrush.

Make off-road practice more formal by setting up a dirt criterium course with sharp corners, fast downhills, and other tough conditions. You will get a feel for your limits on the bike, and the physical penalties for a mistake are not as severe as on pavement. And it's fun as well as instructional. Those prairie dogs are pretty quick.

It's smart to wear a layer or two of sweat clothes and your hardshell helmet, of course, to protect yourself when you fall. And you will fall if you are doing this sort of training correctly — you will lean the bike over so far in corners that the rear wheel skids. The reflexes that are developed will carry over into criteriums. If you don't go down occasionally you aren't going to learn your limits and how to come back from the brink of wiping out. Don't be afraid to take chances.

Also, don't neglect to ride in the dirt with others. Bike handling by yourself is one thing, but all the rules change when you are close to other riders who interrupt your line. You must learn to focus not only on the physical act of getting around the corner, but also on the riders moving with you.

The third and most specific technique is to practice on your road bike. Find a half-mile course with as many consecutive corners as possible without traffic signals. A little scouting in suburban areas will probably uncover several possibilities.

For example, I have an ideal course two blocks from my home with five corners in seven-tenths of a mile. One is a fast 90 degrees and another is 120 degrees. Only one has a stop sign and that is at the top of a rise where I'm not going fast enough to practice cornering anyway. Sometimes I sweep the corners before I ride but usually I don't; a little debris in training prepares me for the unexpected in a race. Four of the turns are right-handers so traffic isn't that much of a problem. I do have to be alert, but that simulates the heads-up attitude needed in a race. I ride this course for about 20 minutes at the end of one training ride each week, using fairly low gears and trying to find the limits on the corners.

Here's another technique that works for me. I go to a parking lot after hours and ride in 42x18 around an imaginary criterium course defined by arrows and lines painted on the pavement. The deserted lot gives me the space to turn both ways while the low gear limits speed so I can corner every 10 to 30 yards and get plenty of practice. Also, the low speed makes a crash easier to take. Again, wear protective clothing and ride an old bike to save your good equipment from damage.

Do the parking lot drill in the rain occasionally and with other similarly equipped riders. A restricted-gear criterium with some friends on a short parking lot course will send you to the first race of the season with razor-sharp reflexes. For variety, find a smooth

Criteriums are held rain or shine, so your training should include some wet-weather bike handling. Find out the difference that rain makes in braking, cornering, and jumping. The lead rider in this breakaway group is Frankie Andreu, a 1986 national track champion.

field with short grass and firm ground. Set up a course with traffic cones. Falls will be even easier to take.

Most riders never practice bike handling in the manner I've just described. If you do you will have an advantage. You will have more confidence on the bike, you will be less of a threat to yourself and others, and your chances of doing well in criteriums will improve. When all is said and done, to be competitive you must stay upright. It helps greatly to train in ways that improve specific bike-handling skills.

Racing rules

Now let's turn attention to actual racing. Top riders agree that there are just a few strategic rules to follow, but they usually mean the difference between success and failure.

First rule: Stay near the front. This won't come as a surprise because it applies to all mass-start racing. But it's especially important for criteriums because crashes are more numerous and can quickly ruin your chances for a good finish. Most criteriums go fast from the gun because they are short, and everyone has plenty of adrenaline built up. Despite the initial effort it takes, experienced riders want to get out front and away from congestion. They want to string out the field quickly so that only those who deserve to be in contention will be.

It requires a complete warm-up to be able to ride hard from the gun. This can be a problem at a downtown criterium if other classes are using the course and nearby streets are unsuitable because of glass and traffic. Some riders use rollers or a TurboTrainer. You also need a positive mental attitude. The first 10 laps may be the toughest of the race except for the last one, so be prepared to feel like you can't last the distance at that pace. The speed will usually ease a little during the middle laps, enabling you to recover if you are well trained. However, if you get dropped early it will be a tough battle to get back on. Make up your mind to say near the front. Don't be intimidated by the pace or the reputations of the other riders.

Second rule: Conserve energy after the first frenetic laps. Beginners often waste energy on chases necessitated by inattention. It is tempting to pedal a little slower for a moment or to ease through a corner, but such lapses in effort can cause you to lose 5-10 places in the field. It is easier to fight to maintain position than it is to continually struggle your way back. Although you will be at the front from time to time, don't take monster pulls in hopes of shattering the field. Unless you are clearly superior, all this will do is tire you out while the pack sits on.

Third rule: Give it all you've got when you can gain an advantage by doing so. When the time is right, don't hesitate. Even beginning riders should be assertive and try to control a race occasionally. You may not pull it off, but on the other hand you may surprise yourself.

Let's say that you want to try an attack. Before you charge off, assess your ability and how you feel at the moment. Some new riders tend to overestimate their strength in the heat of the action and try moves that have no chance of success. Other beginners lack confidence and do nothing but sit in. You will learn only by trying to attack and then observing the outcome. Don't be discouraged. Even experienced riders lack the power and riding ability to make many moves stick.

Attacks work best when made from about one-third of the way back in the pack. This will enable you to pass the front riders at fast speed, surprising them and opening a gap. Then be mentally ready to defend your advantage. If you are known as a rider with some strength and your competitors suspect that you could stay away, their chase could be intense.

Another technique is to drift off the front, opening a gap as if by accident. Increase your pace with a minimum display of effort until the pack decides that you pose a threat and the chase begins. When it does, drop all pretense and get on it. This technique is harder than it sounds because it requires a fine sense of timing, careful analysis of how other riders feel, strict self-control, and a touch of acting ability. Experience is the teacher.

Fourth rule: Stay off the pavement. That's common sense, but not so obvious is that bike handling and cornering require strategy as well as skill. All your off-season cornering practice is useless unless you can stay relaxed in a crowd. If you look at some riders in a criterium you'll see white knuckles and straining forearms as they clutch the bars with a death grip. This wastes energy and reduces bike control. Good criterium riders concentrate, in a relaxed way, on one corner at a time.

Cornering is easier from the front. The first several riders can choose the best line for maintaining speed, but later riders have to slow down because the road becomes clogged. Then they must sprint hard merely to catch up, which uses energy and increases the chance of a crash.

Use brakes sparingly. Most fairly flat criterium courses with 90-degree turns don't require braking, but you'd never know it from the squealing of pads on rims in lower-category races. Unnecessary braking has a chain-reaction effect, too. A timid rider who grabs his brakes just before a turn forces everyone behind him to slow abruptly. Once the pattern is established, riders become hesitant in corners. Their uncertainty becomes a fertile climate for crashes.

Finally, learn how to ride the last lap well. If you have the strength and the skill to stay with the leaders, your strategy both in the sprint and in the chaotic action leading up to it will determine your success.

The majority of criteriums come down to either a field sprint or a sprint contested by members of a breakaway. Solo finishes are rare because most courses are too flat to let any one rider escape. When you plan your strategy for any criterium it is wise to figure on winding up in a sprint.

As you ride around the course before the race, check the terrain leading to the finish. Is there a sharp corner close to the line? If so, the first rider through it will probably be the winner. The real sprint will take place on the far side of the course as riders try to get to the front. If you don't realize this, if you save your strength and aggression for the finishing straight, you will lose.

There was a great example of this in the men's Vail Criterium at the '82 Coors Classic. The winding course featured a sharp, narrow corner just 120 meters from the finish, a corner made more treacherous by a concrete pillar right in its center. In early prime hunting Canadian star Steve Bauer caught a pedal there and crashed heavily. Battered and cut, he chased long and hard to get back on. By the end he was in position to challenge Davis Phinney for the win. Despite his painful crash there earlier, Bauer never hesitated but swept sharply through the inside of the final corner and narrowly lost a controversial sprint. Bauer knew that to have a chance he needed to attack that corner, never mind the still-burning abrasions.

The wind can be a major factor, too. Tailwind sprints can sometimes be won from the front, but those that feature a wind in your teeth are best ridden from farther back so you will have some protection. Be careful, though, because everyone will be jockeying for position.

Is there a downhill near the finish? This will increase the speed and serve as a launching platform that quite a few riders will take advantage of. Be prepared for the sudden burst. Don't get caught up in the middle of the pack or you won't have a chance.

Know exactly where you want to be when the final burst begins.

It is the consensus of top riders that fourth or fifth place is best. This provides some room to maneuver and a chance for a good leadout.

If you have a teammate willing to lead you out, take advantage of it. Knowing who will launch you to the line is a lot better than trying to decide whose wheel to follow in that frenzied last lap. At a criterium in Denver one year I latched onto a strong rider who had won the previous day's race with a blistering finish. He rolled it out from 400 meters and I nearly blew my engine to get on his wheel. Once there I congratulated myself on my smart tactics. Then 100 meters from the line he sat up, blocking me while his teammate and half a dozen others shot by. It helps to have someone you can trust up there.

Choose the correct gear for your sprinting style and the conditions. You will go past the finish line plenty of times during the race, so you should get a feel for what gear will work best. Just be careful not to gear too high because you will lose a quick jump. Also, it is easier to shift to a bigger gear than to a smaller one if you do make a mistake. Not many riders can use the 53x13 or 12 in which human rockets like Bauer and Phinney routinely win flat sprints.

After each criterium review your successes and mistakes. If you have a coach or experienced teammate who watched you, get their suggestions and advice. Then work on your weak points starting with next week's training.

24
Road Racing

For those who love the sport
for the challenges it presents

MOST RIDERS GET their introduction to mass-start racing in criteriums, but often it's the long road race that catches their fancy. One reason is the mystique surrounding tough European pro events like Paris-Roubaix and the stages of the major tours. Another is the real thrill of covering 100 miles in about four hours using nothing but human power. Also, road races suit many occasional competitors who prefer long training rides. They neglect speed work so look forward to events where they can showcase their endurance. And since road races generally have more hills and punishing conditions than criteriums, they appeal to the "tough guy" rider (of either sex) who loves the sport for the challenges it presents.

Good road racing skills are a must for the cyclist with hopes of competing internationally. The U.S. has a surplus of criterium flashes who can't climb and don't have the stamina to go 100 tough miles. The Coors Classic reflects our love affair with short-course racing, but general classification is rarely affected by the criterium stages. It is those long, hard grinds over Loveland Pass or around the Morgul-Bismarck course that produce the big time splits.

Most of the criterium techniques I discussed in the last chapter also apply to road racing, but some additional knowledge and skills are required.

Equipment

It is useful to think of bike setup as a continuum ranging from stripped down and exotic, as for time trials, to heavy and reliable, as for training. A road racing bike tends toward the training end. For most events it can be set up about the same as for a criterium, with a few changes dictated by the course and conditions.

Wheels are an important consideration. For road racing, strength is a greater priority than lightness. It does no good to save weight on rims if they are easily dented on railroad tracks. You can lose minutes getting a wheel change or even crash if a damaged rim locks the brakes. Heat-treated rims tend to be heavy, but they are strong and probably worth the additional expense.

Light tires are almost always a bad idea in road racing. You can sometimes get away with 210-gram tubulars in criteriums if the course has been swept, but they won't hold air long out on the open road of patched pavement, potholes, and sharp gravel. Since most road courses aren't closed to traffic, there may be a patch of glittering glass 10 miles from the finish that wasn't there the evening before when the promoter checked the course. Or, as can happen, a driver frustrated by the delay will fling a bottle on the road directly in front of the pack. A little more rubber between that fragile pink tube and debris may be all the margin you need. A 250-gram cotton tire is a good choice for most road conditions.

Most races provide a service vehicle to follow the main pack. It will carry personal wheels and a few sets that anyone can use. Sometimes the people in the vehicle can be classified as spectators more than mechanics, so you may have to do your own wheel change if you puncture. If you have your own spare wheels, be sure to mark them clearly with your name and race number. Use an index card and wedge it between two crossing spokes. With luck, someone in the car will pull out the proper wheel and you will be riding again without losing too much time. Use the arm signals discussed on page 88 and hope for the best. After the service you'll have to go all out to regain the pack, even at the risk of blowing up. It does no good to dangle 30 seconds down for 20 miles.

Some races require that you carry a spare tire and pump. Riders get upset about this because their vision of real bike racing includes a caravan of service vehicles bristling with spare wheels and coldly competent race mechanics schooled in 15-second wheel changes. Unfortunately, U.S. courses are often so crowded with general traffic that the burden of numerous race vehicles could cause the state patrol to deny a road-use permit. If you don't carry a spare, you may have to wait a long time by the side of the road for the broom wagon. But even if you have one, it takes several minutes to change a tire and secondhand glue can't be trusted in bike handling at race speeds. This makes it smart, if not mandatory, to forget the race and ride in for training. Be sure to inflate your spare periodically with the frame pump to be certain both work.

Ask a non-racing friend to go to the event with you. He or she can then drive down the course to find you if something prevents you from finishing. It's not too pleasant being stranded 20 miles from your car, hoping that someone will drive out to rescue you after everyone else has completed the race.

If the finish is miles from the start and you haven't planned ahead, you may have to pedal back to your car without leg warmers or jacket, shivering and exhausted. For example, the Bob Cook Memorial Mt. Evans Hill Climb in Colorado has seen many unprepared racers embark on a treacherous 28-mile descent over sleet-slickened broken pavement after having totally expended themselves on the ascent.

Fluid replacement

Long road races require fluids and, in some cases, food.

The amount of fluid you need will vary depending on the weather. Heat increases the body's demand for water, and the humidity (or lack of it) is often just as important — extremely dry air seems to cause as much of a problem as sultry conditions. In the desert-like atmosphere of the 100-mile Grand Junction-to-McClure Pass stage of the '82 Coors Classic, the dryness sucked the moisture vampire-like from the riders even though the temperature was cool.

Another factor is the speed and intensity of the racing. If everyone goes flat out from the gun and you are barely hanging on, it's hard to drink. If you lose a little speed while handling the bottle you could go off the back. It's difficult to swallow when you are breathing hard, too. Once you get it down, your stomach may rebel. (The ability to vomit while pedaling at 28 m.p.h. is a skill that most riders haven't mastered.) However, fast races drain fluids at a great rate and it is crucial to replace them. Often the pace will ease temporarily. If not, take a quick swallow every few minutes. Don't put it off until you feel thirsty because then it's too late.

While a jersey pocket can be stuffed with sufficient food, it is nearly impossible to carry enough water for some races. You can install an extra bottle cage on your seat tube and carry a third bottle in the jersey, but if you take more than that the weight will make you feel like a tank truck. Instead, plan to get the extra fluids you need at the feed zone.

The feed is usually on a hill because riders are going slower. Standard technique is for the feeder to run along the side of the road ahead of the pack holding out a bottle or musette bag at arm's length. His rider takes it like an old-time freight train picking up the mail. It helps if the feeder wears a team jersey so the rider can pick him out of the crowd.

All kinds of things can go wrong at the feed. Alexi Grewal dropped a much-needed bottle in full view of the CBS cameras late in the Morgul-Bismarck stage of the '82 Coors Classic. It was a conspicuous example of a frequent occurrence. Because riders are leaning, reaching, swerving, and running over dropped items, crashes are common. Attacking through the feed zone is a standard tactic. It helps to be at the front so you can counter any moves as well as avoid congestion.

Climbing tactics

Climbing is a skill that separates the good road racer from the mediocre one. Fitness alone is not enough. You also need to have good technique, but there is no consensus among top riders on what that may be.

Conventional wisdom holds that the larger, more muscular rider should stay seated on long climbs so the bike will support his weight. A light, small-boned rider, on the other hand, will usually prefer to stand and "run" up the mountain. However, it is hill training, not necessarily body size, that should determine how you are most efficient. One way to find out is to time yourself on a certain climb when standing all the way, sitting all the way, and alternating both positions. During several weeks of trials a pattern should become apparent.

Gearing is also an individual matter. Some riders will push a gear at 60 r.p.m. while others prefer a lower gear so they can spin at 90 or so. It is helpful to have at least one gear lower than you think you will need. It may look impressive to roll to the start of a mountainous race sporting a 12-18 cluster, but the psychological impact will get devalued in a hurry when you are plodding up the first hill while others spin past. If you encounter headwinds, are especially tired on the climb because of hard racing just before it, or if you have leg cramps, the emergency low gear will help you maintain.

If you don't know the course be wary of other riders' recommendations. Just because they are comfortable in a 42x19 doesn't mean that you'll be. Some riders always exaggerate the gears they use for reasons of vanity or to trick competitors.

Although technique is important, good climbing is partly mental. Above all don't let your body type influence your perceptions of how good you can be. Big or stocky riders often feel at a disadvantage on long climbs and they envy the lightweights. But Thurlow Rogers beat uphill ace Alexi Grewal for second place in the mountainous Vail Pass stage of the '82 Coors, and he has a build more suited for a defensive back. Don't let preconceived notions interfere with your real ability.

Attacking on hills

A road race in varied terrain provides many more places to attack than the usual criterium. Long climbs, short hills, treacherous turns, wind, and the feed zone all represent opportunity if you are a practiced rider who keeps an eye out for possibilities.

If you are a good climber, force the pace on the hills. You may not get away but you'll take some of the speed out of the road sprinters, open gaps on the criterium and track specialists, and say goodbye to weaker riders who have been barely hanging on.

Sometimes a hard jam up a hill will split the pack. Strong but inattentive riders caught on the wrong side of the gap will waste a lot of energy trying to bridge, and maybe they won't make it. You will have eliminated or at least reduced the strength of some potential challengers.

If you are more a speed merchant than a climber, make your attacks on short rises (sprinter's hills). Jam up these climbs of a half mile or less and use your superior anaerobic ability to drop the aerobic ascenders. You won't get as big a lead as you could on a longer hill, but you may be able to lengthen it on the descent if the extreme exertion has put your opponents into oxygen debt.

Don't despair on long climbs. Many hills tend to go up steeply for a time, flatten out, and then pitch up steeply again. If you are fit you can push hard to stay in contact on the steeper walls and recover a bit in between.

Above all, don't give up if you are dropped on a hill. The leaders may ease later or they may be pure climbers who can't go very fast on the flat in contrary winds. You might be able to link up with other dropped riders and regain contact in more favorable terrain. This isn't farfetched. Ron Hayman won the '82 Coors Classic stage that covered two laps of the Colorado National Monument even though he went off the back both times up the climb. He kept at it and managed to stagger back on when the pace slowed. After the second time he moved to the front on the rolling final miles and was recovered enough to get away with a Czech rider and then outsprint him for the victory. Had Hayman given up either time he was dropped, he would have lost not only

A long grind through difficult terrain is the essence of bicycle road racing. When a small group escapes, such as this one is about to in the Coors Classic, it may leave the peloton far behind. Always race near the front so you will be ready to join a breakaway that has a good chance of success.

the chance to win but many valuable minutes on general classification.

Attacking through turns

Because there are few turns in most road races they are great places to attack. In criteriums everyone rides the same well-swept corners repeatedly and even timid riders develop a feel for how fast they can safely go. A long road course, on the other hand, will probably present turns spiced with potholes, gravel, glass, and other gruesome hazards of the real world. If you have practiced in training, you can get through some pretty gritty turns quickly and open a gap simply on the basis of superior cornering ability.

Unlike in criteriums, on big-loop or point-to-point courses you will see each corner only once. You must develop the ability to know how fast you can go solely by eyeing the corner as you fly toward it. This isn't easy, so most riders are conservative. They figure that there aren't many corners and they can catch up if they do fall behind. However, it takes only one corner for you to escape if you can get around it faster than everyone else.

Position in the field is important. As in criterium cornering it's best to be near the front so you aren't slowed by others or caught in a crash. Getting up there from halfway back in the pack requires a small attack in itself. This may not be possible if it means violating the centerline rule. You can't always be the first rider through turns, but your odds of remaining unscathed decrease in proportion to your distance from the front. Fight for good position so you can take advantage of the opportunities that corners present.

On unfamiliar courses keep an eye down the road for the orange vests of corner marshalls. Before the race, study the map or talk to other riders and officials so you know where to expect turns and hills.

If you get to the corner in front, take a good line and get through it as fast as possible. Leave a small margin for error but be aggressive. As soon as the bike straightens up get out of the saddle and jump hard. Since there aren't many turns in a road race you can gamble the energy on getting away or inspiring a break. If you aren't at the front you will have to jump anyway merely to get back to the leaders. That's a defensive use of energy that can be avoided if you ride smart.

After you jump, stroke hard for 100 yards or so. Then look back under your elbow. If you are alone and want to chance a solo, continue to go hard. If you and several riders have a split, let the next one pull through while you assess their strength and willingness to work. If your jump accomplished nothing and the whole pack is on your wheel, drop back to between fifth and tenth position, recover, and think about trying it again later.

Anytime you hear a crash behind you, accelerate immediately both to get clear of possible involvement and to take advantage of the confusion. Although some riders have a compulsion against attacking after a crash, it is not bad sportsmanship but a perfectly acceptable tactic as long as you didn't intentionally cause it for your benefit. If you are able, through superior ability, to get through the corner upright while others go down, it is ethical to use that superiority to increase your advantage.

Another good place to attack is the feed zone, where confusion usually reigns as riders jockey to get their hand-ups. If you are at the front you can grab your bottle and attack while those behind try to find theirs in the welter of outstretched arms. Another technique is to start with enough water to last the race. Then go when others slow to get resupplied.

Another opportunity comes with the wind. It can be more of a factor in a road race than in a criterium, where you never have to ride against it for more than half a mile or so because of the course layout. Point-to-point road races, on the other hand, may dish up 100 miles of howling headwind.

In a headwind try to get as much shelter as possible from other riders until actually making an escape attempt. Practice your riding technique on windy training days. Some riders try for a low, aerodynamic position to cut wind resistance. Others sit up a bit to get more leverage and breathe with less obstruction.

Your psychological approach to wind is the most important factor. An attack may succeed simply because you believe that you are tougher than the unpleasant conditions. The other riders, thinking that your attack is suicidal, won't take up the chase and you are away.

STAGE RACING

Now that we've examined the skills necessary to ride time trials, criteriums and road races, it's time to look at the event that puts them all together — the stage race. Only top riders have the chance to compete in events like the Tour de France, the Coors Classic or the Milk Race, but most of us can enter a weekend stage race several times each season.

Preparation

Physical preparation for a short stage race requires few changes from normal training. But you do have to be ready to go at race effort at least two days in a row and sometimes twice in one day. Duplicate these demands in training occasionally with back-to-back hard days or double sessions.

If possible, race on both Saturday and Sunday in the weeks before the stage race. Or race Sunday after a hard training ride on Saturday. Be sure you have developed a good mileage base so that consecutive days of all-out effort don't irritate tendons and ligaments. Without a good base, the fatigue from even a three-stage race can linger long past the event and interfere with your improvement.

Stage races can be hard on equipment as well as on your body, so have your bike and spare wheels in top condition. You'll need your tool kit for between-stage repairs. Don't forget extra riding clothes. One rider I know ripped his only pair of shorts in a first-stage crash and had to ride subsequent stages with the tattered rags flapping in the breeze. Even if the weatherman predicts bluebirds and gentle breezes, be prepared for sleet and rain because you will probably get both.

Rest more than normal before a stage race. Take several easy days and a day off to be sure you are physically and mentally ready. Watch your diet during this period and on the way to the race. Some riders order unfamiliar food while traveling and it upsets their system. Still others make a fetish out of carbohydrate loading, but this technique is just about useless for a stage race. Glycogen stores are good only for about a two-hour effort.

Take care of logistics. Make motel reservations in advance and ask about suitable places to eat. Don't waste time and energy searching around an unfamiliar town the night before the start.

Some racers with families consider stage races as weekend vacations, as good reasons to take a trip with the spouse and kids. But if racing is your No. 1 priority make it clear in advance that the event and your rest take precedence over sightseeing.

Racing weekends can be done on a shoestring budget but your performance will likely suffer. The first year I raced, my wife and son often accompanied me and we tried to save money by sleeping in the back of our decrepit VW van. My wife was patient and supportive enough not to complain, but our eight-month-old son had none of the social graces. He knew that the van was cold, the campground noisy, his bed (the car seat) hard, and he had no qualms about crying all night to communicate his distress. My most vivid memory of several stage races that year is of sitting in the driver's seat at 3 a.m., rocking a crying kid while thinking about racing again in several hours.

Racing techniques

Most techniques applicable to one-day events work well for the criteriums, road races, and time trials in short stage races. The main difference is the increased importance of competing with your head as well as your legs.

One essential stage-race skill is the paradoxical ability to parcel out energy through the entire event yet go all out at the right time in individual stages. It takes experience to know how far you can extend yourself and still recover for the next day's racing. You can't find out by racing just once each weekend.

Multiple world champion Jeannie Longo, twice a winner of the world's No. 1 stage race for women, the Coors Classic, knows the value of experience in multiday events. Only by racing on consecutive days will you learn how hard you can push and still recover for the next stage.

"Everyone races differently through the week," says 1984 Olympic Road Race winner Connie Carpenter-Phinney about the Coors Classic, which she won three times. "Some people fade and some get stronger. You just have to know yourself."

Unlikely as it sounds, you will probably feel better in the second and third stages than you do in the first. This is usually because the initial energy-sapping nervousness is overcome.

Try never to use energy indiscriminately. Before the event begins, study the race bible or information sheet and plan your approach. If you are primarily interested in the general classification (GC) avoid doing needless work in criteriums. You could hammer all day at the front but succeed only in becoming fatigued. This will hurt your chances in time trials and road stages where the big time splits take place. However, breaks can gain valuable time even in criteriums and there are often time bonuses for the first several places. You have to constantly evaluate the situation.

In a one-day race you can be daring about joining breaks or demonstrating your strength at the front, but in a stage race you have to consider how such tactics will affect you two days later. On the other hand, the first stage may be the one most likely to decide who will be in contention for the rest of the event. Colorado's Durango-Iron Horse race, a Memorial Day tradition for racers in the Rockies, opens with a 50-mile road race over three passes with about 5,000 feet of climbing. In most categories GC is quickly established since the time that strong climbers gain in the mountains can't be made up in the subsequent criterium and short, rolling road race. Past winners include riders with big engines like George Mount, Bob Cook, Tom Sain, and Jonathan Boyer who used their superior horsepower on the first day.

Mental approach

A positive mental attitude is the most vital factor in stage racing success. Experienced riders know that they will have bad days, that they will feel exhausted or sick. The successful ones have learned to forget each day's performance and concentrate on the next stage. They may be languishing far down in GC but there is always the possibility of making a crucial break and moving up a dozen places.

Stage racing is no place for a rider who worries about things he can't control, or about things he can control but doesn't attend to. All worry does is drain the energy needed for the next stage. Don't fret about that questionable tire, replace it right now. Don't spend hours brooding over a potentially dangerous course. Briefly review how you will ride it and then forget about it until the gun goes off. You can ride well only if you live calmly in the present moment. As the Zen master says, "Be here now."

But no matter how positive your attitude or how extensive your talents, stage racing is going to be tough. Rookie riders are often shocked by the physical demands and hard conditions. Many become depressed at how far they are forced past what they consider safe limits. If you realize this you will be less likely to give up your effort. It's tough for everyone, but if some can succeed you can, too.

Another way you race with your head is to sort out the best long-term move in a stage. This is hard when you are presented with a confusing array of options that will influence both the day's results and GC. At times it can require the memory and calculating ability of a computer to keep track of the dangermen and react correctly to what they are doing, all the while pedaling at 25 m.p.h. or faster.

Unless you are unattached or have no teammates in the race, you need to think about your role as team rider. Most stage races have team prizes based on the accumulated time of each squad's leading riders; for example, the first three when there are five-man squads. Sometimes individual hopes of glory have to be postponed if a teammate has an even better chance of winning. It takes quick thinking to realize this in the middle of a stage, and an unselfish attitude to react correctly for the good of the team.

Another mental demand is having to compete under a special set of rules. Often there are more regulations for a stage race than for the one-day races you are accustomed to. If you don't know the rules you risk being penalized and possibly disqualified. Is there a free-lap rule in the criterium stage? Will you get the same time as the group you were riding with if you crash in the final kilometer?

Finally, remember that a stage race is a high-stress workout that can make you measurably stronger several weeks later. It is also fun and exciting, and this can mask your fatigue with a sense of exhilaration. You may feel enthused to resume hard training as soon as the race is over. Don't do it. You've stressed your body more than usual so ease off for several days to allow recovery. If you do, the stress you've been through can help stimulate a big jump in form.

25
Cycling's Risks
Answering the question: "How can you justify your dangerous sport?"

MY NON-CYCLING FRIENDS think bike racers are crazy. They can't believe how long road races are. If they get on a bike and try to sustain 20 m.p.h. they become exhausted. As a result they are flatly incredulous when I tell them that races go at 25-28 m.p.h. for several hours. Sprinter's hills loom like mountains in their minds and the Bob Cook Memorial Mt. Evans Hill Climb is simply unimaginable. When I assert that the training which brings such performances within reach is enjoyable rather than agonizing, they nod knowingly to one another.

But these doubters reserve their most vehement attacks on my sanity for what they perceive as the unacceptable dangers of cycling. Recently a friend picked up an old copy of a racing publication and read about Alan Kingsbery's near-fatal collision with a truck crossing a time trial course. When he finished he looked at me searchingly. "How can you justify your sport," he asked, "when you have a wife and son?"

I did not consider the question idle, presumptuous or even rhetorical. I have asked it of myself at times, especially after crashes or close calls. Certainly there are safer activities for a person in his 30s who has heavy responsibilities in life. But because I enjoy cycling so much, I find it easy to justify — what dangers there are seem eminently worth the risk. Yet part of me realizes that my justifications are not the real reason I ride in spite of the hazards. Consider how easily I can find excuses to ignore the danger:

•Given the state of automobile accident statistics, I am probably at least as safe when racing, commuting and training as I would be in a car.

•Wearing a hardshell cycling helmet cuts down on the risk of serious injury and fatality. And I wear one at all times, not just when racing.

•We have to take some calculated risks in life. Man is by nature a risk-taker, a challenger of limits, or he would not have evolved. In fact, the whole evolutionary history of life is a history of the risks that nature takes when minute individual differences are introduced into the species. Many of these fail, but some are successful and lead to improved adaptation to the challenges of life. In the same way, an individual human life without risk would result in a stagnant personality. Thoreau was right: When it comes time for me to die, I do not want to look back on my life and find that I have not lived.

•Racing helps me to stay fit. The alternative, a sedentary lifestyle, is more deadly than any danger faced while cycling. Of course, I could get fit by swimming, but I have no talent for it — I would probably drown (that really is an unjustifiable risk). Serious running, for me, is unhealthy. My knees can rarely handle runs over 20 miles and my hips get sore at random, apparently just to be contrary. Although it may be argued that I could maintain my fitness by recreational cycling and avoid the sport's dangers, I see commuting, training and racing as part of the whole experience. Each reinforces and gives meaning to the others until the composite attitude toward transportation, health, enjoyment and competition merges into a lifestyle.

•I am safer in cycling than in other sports I could choose. I played football enthusiastically and with abandon for 10 years, but the major injury and death statistics from that sport continue to appall me. After college I got involved in mountaineering. I still have recurring visions of a basketball-size boulder bounding at me down a couloir on Crestone Needle. It missed; my knees shook for an hour. When I downhill ski it is either me or the mountain and I've never won yet. I could become a motorcycle racer, a cliff diver, a Pipeline surfer or an Indy driver. In comparison to many sports, not to mention wars or everyday household accidents, cycling is outrageously safe.

Even though all these arguments roll glibly off my tongue, responsibility to family remains a disturbing and pertinent point. However, I would rather take a small and calculated risk to be a fit, alive, interesting and exuberant cyclist than come ponderously home each evening to the TV and snack tray. The risks of such a lifestyle may be less obvious than those of racing, but they are more insidious, more deadly and, to my mind, far less acceptable. In the end I can easily justify my cycling: We cannot choose the time and manner of our deaths, but we can have a say in the style and quality of our lives.

But to list reasons why I can accept the dangers of cycling is merely to eliminate the negative. Trying to justify cycling by checking off the debits ignores the positive reasons for racing and training that overwhelm the drawbacks.

My reasons for racing do not arise out of a simplistic view of competition. I rarely taste the thrill of victory; as for the agony of defeat, I try to keep my performances in proper perspective. Racing is certainly not my whole life nor do I wish it to be. When I am honest with myself I realize that I race for three reasons, all compelling, but none noble or unselfish.

I race because I hate pain. I know that such an admission, besides sounding like a paradox, is inconsistent with the cliche of the macho cyclist picking gravel out of grisly abrasions while gritting his teeth on a spare crankset bolt, but it is true. The longer I have been involved in sports, the more fascinated I have been by my reaction to pain. I have become addicted to the process of facing that pain and trying to beat my fear and loathing. The result is now a post-race euphoria that is only slowly replaced by accelerating anxiety about the next contest. Aristotle may not have been a bike racer but he knew about fear and pain. He called it catharsis: a combination of pity, terror and relief. He was talking about the audience's reaction to tragedy, but it is applicable to us moderns as we experience self-inflicted "sports-pain" — pity for ourselves at the spectre of approaching pain, terror that it will hurt so much we'll quit or slow down and get dropped, and finally relief that the demon has been met face to face and conquered, or at least confronted honestly. In the weekly cycle of quiescence, anxiety, competition and catharsis, my fear and hatred of pain is purged.

I also race because I like to ride with other people — sometimes. Since I live far from the area where most of Colorado's races and riders are located I usually train alone. I prefer it that way because I can ride when it fits my schedule. But part of the thrill of cycling is how bikes handle around other bikes: the vacuum, suction, lightening sensation of a big pack, the psychedelic patterns of alloy and jerseys, the sense of shared enterprise and momentary alliances, the way the pack develops a mind and will of its own, independent of, and yet connected to, each rider's perceptions and personality. Nowhere is this better experienced than in a race where individuals merge into one sinuous group while still maintaining their separate wills and motivations and personalities. When I train alone I clear my head of all the trivia of the day. But when I am in a pack of riders I feel a part of the race, sharing the hopes, dreams and honest fears of everyone else.

Finally, I like to ride and racing gives me an excuse to do it often. I don't need to justify my riding to other people, but when daily tasks press hard on the time I set aside for me, it helps to be able to justify it to myself.

I like to ride in the autumn when the mountains are magnified in the clear air until I can see every rock on Wetterhorn Peak 40 miles away; when the air at dawn rings like china.

In spring, when the wind blows from the southwest, I rise at dawn to beat it. Hunched over the bars I sense birdsong blown past my ear and acrid smoke blowing in veils across the road. A farmer, burning off irrigation ditches, leans splay-legged on his shovel and stares as I ride by. I can hear him at supper: "I saw that young fella on the bicycle again, Mabel. Don't that beat all?"

Summer — cool at dawn, dry heat shimmering from the roads by noon. Bugs rattle off my helmet on downhills and the jersey pockets are full of spare bottles. The roads choke with pickup campers and cars bearing flatland license plates, the tourists gaping at the mountains.

And winter, my favorite. I ride off the mesa into town in the 15 F degree morning, the chill factor stinging my chest through three layers of jerseys and two editions of the local paper. By the return trip the day's new snow has been pushed to the side of the road and there are cars headed to Aspen, Telluride and Crested Butte with skis on racks and incredulous looks behind frosted windshields. My nose drips. At home I lift weights while gathering clouds coalesce above the Uncompahgre Plateau and spit their first flakes of snow.

How can I justify my racing when I have a wife and child? In the final analysis it is the time spent away from them while training and racing that enables me to return changed — added to somehow by the experience, made more than when I left. And that, it seems to me, is justification enough.

AFTERWORD

U.S. Cycling Federation

The governing body of American amateur bicycle racing is the U.S. Cycling Federation, a not-for-profit corporation with roots dating to 1920. Among its functions are the establishment and enforcement of racing rules, the sanctioning of events and licensing of competitors. Even first-time racers must have a USCF license in order to ride in a sanctioned event, unless the promoter includes a race for "novices." The annual fee of $32 is applicable to all riders except those aged 13 or under who pay $16. Licensed riders are sent a copy of the USCF rule book and issues of the federation's monthly publication, *Cycling USA*. A rider's class for the year is determined by his or her age on January 1. Class and age groups for men and women are: Junior 9-13, Junior 14-15, Junior 16-17, Senior 18-34, Senior 35-44, Senior 45-54, and Senior 55-plus.

The Senior Men class is by far the largest and it is subdivided into four categories based on ability and experience. A first-time license holder aged 18-34 will be placed in Senior Category IV and must remain there until earning the right to upgrade to Category III. This is accomplished by placing in the top three in three qualifying road events, in the top six in six, or simply by competing in eight or more sanctioned races. But since many promoters merge IVs and IIIs into a single race there is little difference between these categories; the real change comes when upgrading from Category III to II. Both the distance of races and quality of competition then become much greater, especially since IIs and Is are often lumped together. A Senior Category I is an elite racer with the potential to contest for national championships and represent the U.S. in foreign competition.

A license application can be requested by writing to the USCF, 1750 E. Boulder St., Colorado Springs, CO 80909. Include $5 if you would like a rule book so you can learn more about the organization of the sport and how races are structured before you decide to take the plunge. Remember that all racing licenses expire on December 31 no matter when during the year they were purchased.

Track Racing

There is another side of cycling competition not dealt with in this book — track racing. It offers some of the fastest, most exciting and varied events in the sport but, unfortunately, the opportunity to participate is limited by the country's low number of velodromes. However, if you do live within reach of one of the tracks listed below I encourage you to attend a meet. You will see some great racing action and find out about training programs and events for beginners. Time spent in a fixed gear on the high bankings will directly improve such road racing skills as pedal action, sprinting and bike handling, and you may discover a real talent for one or more of the events. The USCF holds District and National Championships for track events just as it does the road.

Alkek Velodrome, Houston, TX. Joe Bentley, 3820 South Shepherd Drive, Houston, TX 77098.

Alpenrose Velodrome, Portland, OR. Mike Murray, 1632 Birdsdale Ave., Gresham, OR 97030.

Balboa Park Velodrome, San Diego, CA. San Diego Velodrome Committee, 2221 Morley Field Drive, San Diego, CA 92104.

Baton Rouge Velodrome, Baton Rouge, LA. 3140 N. Sherwood Forest Blvd., Baton Rouge, LA 70809.

Brown Deer Velodrome, Milwaukee, WI. Milwaukee Wheelmen, 2607 N. Downer, Milwaukee, WI 53211.

Dick Lane Velodrome, East Point, GA. Michael Hoffland, Director, Dick Lane Velodrome, 1431 Norman Berry Drive, East Point, GA 30344.

Dorais Velodrome, Detroit, MI. Wolverine Sports Club, Box 63, Royal Oak, MI 48068.

Encino Velodrome, Encino, CA. Southern California Cycling Federation, Box 713, Torrance, CA 90508.

Kissena Velodrome, Kissena, NY. Al Toefield, Track Chairman, 87-66 256th St., Floral Park, NY 11001.

Lehigh County Velodrome, Trexlertown, PA. Lehigh County Velodrome, 217 Main St., Emmaus, PA 18049.

Madison Velodrome (portable), Harper Woods, MI. Velodrome Inc., 19386 Kelly Road, Harper Woods, MI 48225.

Major Taylor Velodrome, Indianapolis, IN. Chuck Quast, 3649 Cold Springs Road, Indianapolis, IN 46222.

Marymoor Velodrome, Redmond, WA. Washington State Bicycling Association, 6714 28th NE, Kirkland, WA 98033.

Meadowhill Park Velodrome, Northbrook, IL. Velodrome, 1710 Pfingsten Road, Northbrook, IL 60062.

Penrose Velodrome, St. Louis, MO. Chester Nelson, 4701 Natural Bridge Road, St. Louis, MO 63115.

Santa Clara County Velodrome, San Jose, CA. San Jose Bicycle Club, Box 973, Los Altos, CA 94022.

7-Eleven Olympic Velodrome, Carson, CA. Velodrome, 1000 E. Victoria St., Carson, CA 90747.

7-Eleven Olympic Training Center Velodrome, Colorado Springs, CO. Fred Cappy, Velodrome Director, USCF, 1750 E. Boulder St., Colorado Springs, CO 80909.

Washington Park Velodrome, Kenosha, WI. Kenosha Wheelmen, 1515 15th Ave., Kenosha, WI 53140.

Glossary

aerobic — an intensity of exercise below the level which produces lactic acid faster than the body can dispose of it. Thus, oxygen needs are continuously met and the exercise can be continued for long periods.

aerodynamic — a design of cycling equipment or a riding position that reduces wind resistance.

attack — an aggressive, high-speed jump away from other riders.

anaerobic — an intensity of exercise past the point where the body can cope with its production of lactic acid and need for oxygen. Thus, the exercise level cannot be sustained for long.

anaerobic threshold — the point at which the body is working so hard it can't supply enough oxygen to keep muscle cells operating efficiently. A by-product of this inefficient metabolism is lactic acid.

blocking — legally impeding the progress of riders in the pack to allow teammates in the break a better chance of success.

blow up — to suddenly be unable to continue at the required pace due to overexertion.

bonk — a state of severe exhaustion caused mainly by the depletion of glycogen in the muscles. Once it occurs, there is no means of quick recovery.

bottom bracket — the part of the frame where the crank is installed.

break, breakaway — a rider or group of riders who have escaped the pack.

bridge, bridge a gap — to catch a rider or group which has opened a lead.

bunch — the main cluster of riders in a race. Also called the group, pack, field and peloton.

butted tube — a type of tubing found in expensive bike frames, the metal being very thin throughout except at each end where it thickens to provide the needed strength at tube intersections.

cadence — the rate of pedaling, measured in revolutions per minute of one foot.

carbohydrates — simple sugars and starches which provide a quick source of muscle energy. They are plentiful in fruits, grains, potatoes, breads, pasta, etc., and are stored in the liver in the form of glycogen.

cardiovascular — pertaining to the heart and blood vessels.

categories — the division of USCF classes into smaller groups, based on ability and/or experience.

chasers — those who are trying to catch a group or a lead rider.

chondromalacia — a serious knee injury in which there is disintegration of cartilage surfaces due to improper tracking of the kneecap. Symptoms start with deep knee pain and a crunching sensation during bending.

circuit — a road course which is ridden two or more times to compose the race.

class — the divisions of USCF racers based on sex and age. Also, something a talented pedaler is said to have.

cleat — a metal or plastic fitting on the sole of a cycling shoe with a groove to engage the rear of torts work in shoes to help neutralize biomechanical imbalances in the feet or legs.

clinchers — conventional tires with a separate inner tube.

cluster, block — a freewheel.

criterium — a mass-start race covering numerous laps of a course that is normally about one mile or less in length.

cyclocross — a fall or winter event contested in part off the paved road. Courses include obstacles, steps and steep hills which force riders to dismount and run with their bikes across their shoulder.

depression insomnia — a symptom of overtraining characterized by ease in falling asleep at night but a period of wakefulness in the early morning hours.

drafting — taking advantage of the windbreak (slipstream) created by another rider. Also called sitting in and wheelsucking.

drops — the part of the handlebars below the brake levers. Also called "hooks."

ergometer — a stationary, bicycle-like device with adjustable pedal resistance used in physiological testing and as an indoor training aid.

fartlek — the Swedish word meaning "speed play," it is a training technique based on unstructured changes in pace and intensity. It can be used in lieu of timed or measured intervals if the rider has the self-discipline to work hard enough.

field sprint — the dash for the finish line by the main group of riders.

fixed gear — a direct-drive setup using one chainwheel and one rear cog, as on a track bike. When the rear wheel turns so does the chain and crank; coasting isn't possible.

glucose — a sugar, the final energy-producing fuel of the cells.

glycogen — a sequence of glucose molecules which make the principal carbohydrate storage material in the body.

hammer — to jam.

hoods — rubber coverings for the brake levers which improve hand comfort.

intervals — a structured method of training which alternates relatively hard, short efforts with recovery periods of easier riding.

jam — a period of hard riding.

jump — a quick, hard acceleration.

lactic acid — a by-product of hard exercise that accumulates in the muscles and causes pain and fatigue.

leadout — a race tactic in which a rider accelerates to his maximum speed for the benefit of a teammate in tow. The second rider then leaves the draft and sprints past him at even greater speed near the finish line.

LSD — long, steady distance. A training technique which calls for continuous rides of at least two hours, done entirely at a firm aerobic pace.

mass start — events such as road races and criteriums in which all contestants line up together and leave the starting line at the same time.

maximal oxygen consumption (max VO2) — the maximum amount of oxygen that a person can consume in one minute. It is basically determined by heredity and is an indicator of potential performance in endurance sports.

minuteman — in a time trial, the rider who is one place in front of you in the starting order. So called because in most TTs riders start on one-minute intervals.

motorpace — riding behind a motorcycle or other vehicle that breaks the wind.

orthotics — custom-made supports work in shoes to help neutralize biomechanical imbalances in the feet or legs.

overgear — using a gear that is too big for current conditions or fitness.

overtraining — deep-seated fatigue, both physical and mental, caused by training at a volume higher than that to which the body can adapt.

oxygen debt — the amount of oxygen that needs to be consumed to pay back the deficit incurred by anaerobic work.

pace line — a single-file group formation in which each rider takes a turn breaking the wind at the front before pulling off, dropping back to the rear position and riding in the others' draft until at the front once again.

peak — a relatively short period of time during which maximum performance can be achieved.

prime — a special award given to the leader on selected laps during a criterium or the first rider to reach a certain landmark in a road race. It is used to heighten the action. Pronounced "preem."

pull, pull through — take a turn at the front.

pull off — to move to the side after riding in the lead so that another rider can come to the front.

pusher — a rider who pedals in a large gear at a relatively slow cadence, relying on the gear size for speed.

quadriceps — the large muscle in front of the thigh, the strength of which helps determine a cyclist's ability to pedal with power.

repetition — each hard effort in an interval workout.

road bike — a bicycle with a freewheel, derailleurs and brakes.

road race — a mass-start race that goes from point to point, covers one large loop or is held on a circuit longer than those used for criteriums.

road rash — any skin abrasion resulting from a fall.

rollers — an indoor training device that works like a treadmill for bikes.

set — in interval or weight training, a specific number of repetitions.

silks — expensive, very light racing tires constructed with silk threads in the casing.

snap — the ability to accelerate quickly.

specificity — the basic law of athletic training that says you get good at those things you practice.

speed work — fast training using techniques like intervals and motorpacing.

spinner — a rider who pedals in a moderate gear at a relatively fast cadence, relying on pedal r.p.m. for speed.

stage race — a multi-day event consisting of point-to-point and circuit road races, time trials and, sometimes, criteriums. The winner is the rider with the lowest elapsed time for all stages.

stayer — a rider with the ability to pedal at a relatively high speed for a long period. Also called a pacer.

straight block — a freewheel with cogs that increase in size in one-tooth increments.

suppleness — a quality of highly conditioned leg muscles that allows a rider to pedal at high cadence with smoothness and power.

team time trial (TTT) — a race against the clock with two or more riders working together.

tempo — hard riding at a fast cadence.

time trial (TT) — a race against the clock in which individual riders start at set intervals and cannot give aid or receive it from others on the course.

tops — the part of the handlebars between the stem and the brake levers.

training effect — the result of exercise done at an intensity and duration sufficient to bring about positive physiological changes. These include increased lung capacity, increased number and size of blood vessels, increased maximal oxygen consumption, reduction of body fat, improved muscle tone, increased blood volume, lowered resting pulse, etc.

tubular or sew-up — a lightweight racing or training tire which has the tube permanently sewn inside the casing. The tire is glued onto the rim.

turnaround — the point where the riders reverse direction on an out-and-back time trial course.

USCF — United States Cycling Federation, the organization in charge of amateur bicycle racing in America. It is affiliated with the UCI and the USOC.

U.S. PRO — U.S. Professional Racing Orgnization, the organization in charge of professional bicycle racing in America. It is affiliated with the UCI.

velodrome — a banked track for bicycle racing.

wind up — steady acceleration to an all-out effort.

Bibliography

Following are a few of the many helpful books available for further information on bicycle racing, bike maintenance, physiology, diet and the activities that help make up a good winter program for cyclists: weight training, running and cross-country skiing.

- Anderson, Robert. *Stretching*. Box 1002, Englewood, CO 80110. 1975.
- Borysewicz, Eddie. *Bicycle Road Racing*. Brattleboro, VT: *Velo-news*, 1985.
- Burke, Edmund. *Science of Cycling*. Champaign, IL: Human Kinetics, 1986.
- Burke, Edmund. *Toward an Understanding of Human Performance*. Ithaca, NY: Movement Publications, 1977.
- Burke, Edmund. *The Two-wheeled Athlete*. Brattleboro, VT: *Velo-news*, 1986.
- Caldwell, John. *The Cross-Country Ski Book*. Brattleboro, VT: Stephen Greene Press, 1981.
- *Complete Guide to Bicycle Maintenance and Repair*. Emmaus, PA: Rodale Press, 1986.
- *Cycling*. Central Sports School (CONI). Rome, Italy: 1972.
- DeLong, Fred. *DeLong's Guide to Bicycles and Bicycling: The Art and Science*. Radnor, PA: Chilton, 1978.
- Fixx, James. *The Complete Book of Running*. New York: Random House, 1977.
- *Food for Fitness*. Mountain View, CA: World Publications, 1975.
- *Inside the Cyclist*. Brattleboro, VT: *Velo-news*, 1979.
- Kolin, M. and D. de la Rosa. *The Custom Bicycle*. Emmaus, PA: Rodale Press, 1979.
- Kolin, M. and D. de la Rosa. *Understanding, Maintaining and Riding the Ten-Speed Bicycle*. Emmaus, PA: Rodale Press, 1979.
- Matheny, Fred. *Solo Cycling*. Brattleboro, VT: *Velo-news*, 1986.
- Matheny, Fred and Stephen Grabe. *Weight Training for Cyclists*. Brattleboro, VT: *Velo-news*, 1986.
- Mirkin, G. and M. Hoffman. *The SportsMedicine Book*. Boston: Little, Brown and Co., 1978.

•Osler, Tom. *Serious Runner's Handbook*. Mountain View, CA: World Publications, 1978.

•Reynolds, Bill. *Complete Weight Training Book*. Mountain View, CA: World Publications, 1976.

•Simes, Jack. *Winning Bicycle Racing*. Chicago: Contemporary Books, Inc., 1976.

Periodicals

•*Bicycle Guide*, 711 Boylston St., Boston, MA 02116. Covers all aspects of bicycle riding and equipment. Nine issues per year.

•*Bicycling*, 33 E. Minor St., Emmaus, PA 18049. Covers all aspects of bicycle riding and equipment. Ten issues per year.

•*Cycling USA*, c/o U.S. Cycling Federation, 1750 E. Boulder St., Colorado Springs, CO 80909. Official USCF publication sent to all licensed riders and also available by subscription. Twelve issues per year.

•*Cyclist*, 20916 Higgins Ct., Torrance, CA 90501. Covers all aspects of bicycle riding and equipment. Nine times per year.

•*Velo-news*, Box 1257, Brattleboro, VT 05301. Photos, news articles and features about national and international racing, including calendar of events and results. Eighteen issues per year.

•*Winning*, 1127 Hamilton St., Allentown, PA 18102. Articles, photos and features about international and professional racing. Twelve issues per year.

GEAR RATIO CHART
Number of teeth on rear sprocket

	13	14	15	16	17	18	19	20	21	22	23	24	25
40	83.1	77.1	72.0	67.5	63.5	60.0	56.8	54.0	51.4	49.1	47.0	45.0	43.2
41	85.2	79.1	73.8	69.2	65.1	61.5	58.3	55.3	52.7	50.3	48.1	46.1	44.3
42	87.2	81.0	75.6	70.9	66.7	63.0	59.7	56.7	54.0	51.5	49.3	47.3	45.4
43	89.3	82.9	77.4	72.6	68.3	64.5	61.1	58.0	55.3	52.8	50.5	48.4	46.4
44	91.4	84.9	79.2	74.3	69.9	66.0	62.5	59.4	56.6	54.0	51.7	49.5	47.5
45	93.5	86.8	81.0	75.9	71.5	67.5	63.9	60.8	57.9	55.2	52.8	50.6	48.6
46	95.5	88.7	82.8	77.6	73.1	69.0	65.4	62.1	59.1	56.5	54.0	51.8	49.7
47	97.6	90.6	84.6	79.3	74.6	70.5	66.8	63.4	60.4	57.7	55.2	52.9	50.8
48	99.7	92.6	86.4	81.0	76.2	72.0	68.2	64.8	61.7	58.9	56.3	54.0	51.8
49	101.8	94.5	88.2	82.7	77.8	73.5	69.6	66.1	63.0	60.1	57.5	55.1	52.9
50	103.8	96.4	90.0	84.4	79.4	75.0	71.1	67.5	64.3	61.4	58.7	56.3	54.0
51	105.9	98.4	91.8	86.1	81.0	76.5	72.5	68.8	65.6	62.6	59.9	57.4	55.1
52	108.0	100.3	93.6	87.8	82.6	78.0	73.9	70.2	66.9	63.8	61.0	58.5	56.2
53	110.1	102.2	95.4	89.4	84.2	79.5	75.3	71.5	68.1	65.0	62.2	59.6	57.2
54	112.2	104.1	97.2	91.1	85.8	81.0	76.7	72.9	69.4	66.3	63.4	60.8	58.3

Number of teeth on front chainring

Index